Till Death Do Us Part

(Unless I Kill You First)

A Step-By-Step Guide
for Resolving Relationship Conflict

iv

Jamie Turndorf, Ph.D.

Till Death Do Us Part

(Unless I Kill You First)

A Step-By-Step Guide
for Resolving Relationship Conflict

LoveQuest Publishing
Millbrook, NY

LoveQuest Publishing
P.O. Box 475
Millbrook, NY 12545

p. cm.
Includes bibliographical references.
ISBN 1-4392-2520-6
ISBN 978-1-4392-2520-2

First published in hardcover in 2000 by Henry Holt and
Company

First Owl Books Edition 2001

Cover designed by Jennifer James

Printed in the United States of America

10   9   8   7   6   5   4   3   2   1

To Jean Pin, my husband,
who has faithfully stood beside me
through life's ups and downs.
Your love, level of acceptance,
and ongoing devotion to our relationship
are the greatest gifts of my life.

♡ ♡ ♡

A woman died and appeared before Saint Peter at the gates of heaven. "What must I do to enter heaven?" the woman asked.

Saint Peter replied, "Very simple. You need only spell one word....*Love*."

"That's easy...l-o-v-e."

With that, the pearly gates parted and she entered heaven.

Saint Peter then said, "Listen, I have to visit the men's room. Would you watch the gate for me...and remember, if anyone wants to enter, make sure that he or she spells the word." Saint Peter left and, one minute later, the woman's husband appeared at the gate.

"What are you doing here?" the woman asked him.

He replied, "I was so heartbroken when you died, that I died instantly. What do I need to do to get in?"

The woman replied, "It's simple. You just need to spell one word."

"What's the word?" he asked.

"Czechoslovakia."

W. T. Triller

Contents

Acknowledgments

Many thanks to Kathy Ronk, my publicist from Amodeo Productions; Kathleen Velletri, who edited the text for typos; the entire staff of Millbrook Library, who cheerfully assisted in obtaining reference materials; Jennifer Taylor James who did an excellent redesign of the book jacket despite a tight deadline; and photographer Diana Elliott for her artfully rendered cover photo.

Preface

Even though this book is designed to help married couples resolve chronic fighting, the principles and techniques presented can be applied to unmarried and gay couples, as well as to relationships between parents and children, siblings, and friends.

I want to also remind you that the generalizations I make about male/female behavior are based upon statistical tendencies. This means that, according to statistical data, a certain behavior is most often displayed by a specific gender. For example, more women than men are emotionally expressive. Don't be surprised if you find that certain generalizations don't fit your particular circumstance. In fact, you may note that your experience is the exact opposite of a statistical finding. No problem. If you need to reverse the gender, in order for my remarks to fit, that's fine. In any case, you will find that the techniques for resolving your conflicts still apply.

You will also notice that I have addressed many passages of this book to women (the "relationship watchdogs" in our society). Since women tend to notice relationship problems first, they are generally the ones who not only initiate conflict discussions but also pursue these discussions in an effort to achieve resolution.

As you read on, you will discover that the success of a conflict discussion depends largely on the way that discussion is initiated and overseen. For this reason, I spend a good deal of time outlining the right and wrong ways to not only begin the discussion, but also how to see it through to a successful resolution. These recommendations mean that you will need to shift how you handle your conflict discussions. Many women balk at the idea that they must do all the work. My answer is simple. I don't care if a woman, a man, a hermaphrodite, or a monkey initiates the conflict discussions; all I care about is that your discussions are handled properly. Since it is generally women who take charge of these discussions, we must face the fact that we are already doing the lion's share of the work. As long as you're doing the work, why not do it properly and effectively?

While your success requires that you make some shifts, I don't want you to think that your partner is getting off unscathed. On the contrary, your partner will be expected to make extraordinary changes in the way he listens and responds to your communications; and by the time you're finished with this program, you'll be amazed at how much he has changed.

On a related note, I want you to be aware that even if the person you are fighting with doesn't engage in the program with you, you will still be able to improve your relationship even if you, yourself, are the only one who makes an effort to alter your way of behaving and responding. Like a pebble cast into a pond, your changes alone will have a profound ripple effect upon your relationship. So don't hesitate to roll up your sleeves and be the one to cast the first stone.

And, finally, while the stories contained in this book are based on true cases, the names have been changed to protect the identities of the people who have shared their lives with me.

Till Death Do Us Part

(Unless I Kill You First)

Introduction

Every couple wants love, endless love. For most of us, love is a joining of the mind and heart, which includes physical attraction, admiration of our spouse's personal qualities and a wish to share together (to hike, swim, watch movies). Love also includes a commitment to your partner's happiness, health, and well-being, as well as a desire to satisfy each other's wishes, needs, requests, and so on. I don't need to go on. You know what love is.

If you are like most people, you loved your mate when you said, "I do." You also vowed to sustain that love, "Till death do us part." So, why is it that many couples fall out of love? Because, in spite of their basic love and emotional fusion at the beginning of their relationship, lovers constitute two different persons whose needs and wishes do not always perfectly match. These differences often lead to overt conflict and fighting over any subject you can imagine, large or small.

Divorce and domestic violence have reached epidemic proportions, and since chronic marital distress is usually a precursor of divorce, and often violence, a program for conflict resolution is needed now more than ever. Millions of conflicted couples (as well as anyone wishing to maintain harmonious relationships) will benefit from my down to earth, easy to apply program for ending fighting. The escape routes, safety valves, and real answers are basic relationship survival tools.

But don't wait to put these tools to work, because fighting only worsens with time. How do I know? I am popularly known as Dr. Love, and through my Center for Emotional Communication, and my world wide web site, "Ask Dr. Love," I have helped millions of couples improve their relationships.

In fact, out of my Center, I have spent nearly twenty five years conducting research with couples suffering from chronic fighting, and my research has produced one of the first proven methods for ending fighting for over 90 percent of the people who use it. This book contains the elements of my conflict resolution program and, if you take the time to apply my principles, you too will break the cycle of destructive fighting.

You may be wondering why you don't already know how to resolve your conflicts. Think about where your formal learning occurred. At school, of course, where you were taught math and English. But what about that course on how to handle your relationships? Zippo. It is a tragedy that no education is offered in this area, considering that we spend more waking hours in interaction with people than we do performing math calculations.

Isn't it about time we went to love school? Or maybe I should say conflict school, because love and hate are blood relatives and love cannot survive unless its first cousin, anger, is properly handled. In fact, unresolved anger is the number one killer of love.

Even if your love is on the firing line; if hate and anger are holding your marriage or intimate relationship hostage, don't despair. Contrary to popular belief, you can rekindle the love you felt in the early days of your relationship. But, you must work at it. It sounds very unromantic, I know. But leaving your relationship to chance, and ending up divorced or estranged is even more unromantic.

The following is a brief overview of the contents of this book.

My program to end relationship fighting begins with a series of preparatory or Cool-Down steps, discussed in chapters 1 through 7, that must be mastered before you can attempt conflict resolution.

I first explain that heated fighting creates a chemical imbalance in men that triggers an involuntary fleeing reaction. When men withdraw from conflict discussions, women become more angry, and conflict escalates. Understanding the chemistry of conflict is the first Cool-Down step.

I next outline the most common subjects of conflict, explain what causes conflict to turn into all-out fighting, and help you figure out whether you are suffering from out-of-control relationship warfare. I then identify the Fight Traps (dysfunctional fighting patterns) and faulty conflict resolution tactics that heat the relationship climate and must be eliminated.

I go on to explain that sexual fights result from three main factors: a man's failure to meet his partner's emotional needs; a lack of understanding of the differences between male and female sexuality; and nonsexual issues being played out in the sexual arena. And I show you how to resolve the sexual fights that stem from each of these three causes.

I next explain that unrecognized Old Scars from childhood fuel relationship fighting. I help identify these early wounds and show how to heal them through the relationship.

After discussing the fact that distressed couples are prone to negatively distorting each other's communication, I show you how to train your mind to fight for you not against you. Conflict resolution cannot occur until distortions are eliminated.

The last preparatory chapter provides specific Climate Control techniques that will cool down your interactions.

The second part of the book presents my proven conflict-resolution program. I show you how to master the essential listening skills; how to identify and resolve nonnegotiable issues; and finally how to resolve your conflicts through the negotiation process.

I don't need to wish you good luck as you embark on this journey with me, because relationship success is not a matter of luck. It comes from learning the simple techniques described in this book and putting them into practice each day. The people who I have worked with and who have followed my program are enjoying happy relationships today. Now it's your turn.

1

Understanding the Chemistry of Fighting

Your husband just informed you that he will be taking a white water rafting trip with his buddies the following weekend. He smiles with boyish delight, displaying a full set of sparkling teeth, which you have to resist punching out. You have asked him, more times than you can remember, to talk with you before making plans. He forgot, clearly a case of juvenile Alzheimer's. Now, you find yourself telling him, once again, how annoyed you are. Suddenly, his eyes glaze over and he turns stone deaf. He's not listening, so you turn up the heat. No use. Instead of understanding what's bugging you, he digs in his heels. This annoys you even more, so you crank up your emotional thermostat. But, before you have finished, he orbits from the room and you are shouting to the back of his head.

Now, you're ballistic. So you chase him to the living room, where you find him staring blindly into space, his jaw tight. You nag, whine, complain, and yell, but he ignores you.

The longer he maintains his stony silence, the more upset you become (he doesn't even love you enough to respond to your pleas). In a last-ditch effort, you push your attack to the max and hammer harder. Eureka! His silence is broken, but instead of offering words of understanding, he hurls verbal death blows.

"Maybe you're the freakin' problem!" he shouts, swinging his fist like a club.

"Don't try to pin this on me....You're the one who made plans to go off."

"Who would want to spend time with a bitch?"

In seconds, he is orbiting from the house.

The next time you try to talk to him about your issue, you're even hotter than last time. And, big surprise: he's more deaf, and more defensive or just plain outta there in the flash of a firefly.

The scenario described above—male retreat under fire—is also referred to as "husband withdrawal"—an involuntary fleeing reaction that occurs when a man feels attacked. And, according to extensive research, husband withdrawal is the number one cause of marital conflict and divorce.

Husband withdrawal is caused by a collision of two incompatible modes of handling conflict: that of the wife, who intensely expresses her hurt and anger and that of the husband who withdraws from the confrontation. The technical name for this phenomenon is the *Demand/Withdraw Negative Escalation Cycle*, and I shall discuss in chapter 7 how women can break this cycle by cooling down their emotional communications. But for now, we must concentrate on the reasons why men withdraw.

According to J. M. Gottman and R. W. Levenson's research, husband withdrawal is caused by a biochemical imbalance that occurs when a man feels threatened. When this occurs, a man's autonomic nervous system (the ANS) kicks into high gear. His adrenal glands begin pumping adrenalin, his heart races up to 100 beats per minute (bpm), his muscles become tense, and he is often sweating. Those are the physiological manifestations of ANS arousal; they are automatic, and occur without the mediation of thought.

Men are physiologically hyper reactive to stress, a fact

that has been empirically demonstrated in numerous studies. For example, I conducted a laboratory study in which I assessed husbands' and wives' arousal levels, using a device that measures pulse rate and amount of skin moisture before, during and after a conflictual marital discussion. The results of this study demonstrated that males, but not females, experience ANS arousal during emotionally fraught discussions. Another study, by C. W. Liberson and W. T. Liberson, yielded the finding that when faced with the same stressors, men experienced physiological disturbances, whereas women's internal chemistry remained relatively stable. Another study, by L. J. P. Van Doornen, found that on an exam day, male subjects' experienced biochemical imbalances, whereas females experienced no physiological changes. The studies are clear. Men are more prone to experiencing ANS arousal in response to stress in general and, relationship conflict, in particular.

When ANS arousal occurs, it triggers the fight-flight response, a primitive, survival reaction that arises whenever a person feels emotionally or physically endangered. The instinct to flee in the face of danger derives from ancient times when men were hunters and had to fight ferocious beasts. Imagine a primitive man on a mission to slay a dragon or rustle up some steer. He was out there facing countless life threats and his body had to be up to the task. Out jumped a tiger, and his body switched into the fight-flight mode, an instinctive reaction that guaranteed that he would either fight the tiger or flee for his life. This instinct was necessary to keep the hunter alive.

How does the fight-flight mechanism figure into the most common form of relationship conflict: the Demand/Withdraw cycle? When a women comes at her guy, baring her teeth, berating him with attacks and criticisms, his ANS sees danger. Modern danger is not in the form of ferocious prey; it has evolved into the angry wife or girlfriend. And, modern

10

man is faced with the same dilemma that his primitive ancestors encountered. Fight the enemy or flee.

Since a man doesn't want to physically assault (fight) with his partner, his body sends out signals that cause him to flee, to withdraw. Withdrawal behaviors are exhibited physically, verbally, and psychically. Examples of physical fleeing include leaving the house or the room and/or avoiding contact with mate; verbal fleeing includes making excuses, justifying or denying responsibility, verbal attacking, and counter blaming; and psychic fleeing, when the mind escapes, includes not listening (functional deafness), appearing stone-faced, becoming silent, or avoiding eye contact. It is important to note that all men who experience relationship distress exhibit withdrawal behaviors in one form or another.

While men are no longer hunters, their biological programming and physiological hyper reactivity to danger is still embedded in their physiology. Not aware that her man's fleeing reactions are the result of this programming, a woman becomes more and more enraged that he doesn't care about her and, unwittingly, sets off more biological fire alarms in her partner. The more he withdraws, the hotter she gets, and, in no time, we have chronic fighting.

To make matters worse, when ANS arousal is in high gear it causes another physiological reaction that further intensifies conflict: a man's cognitive functions diminish, which means that reason and logic cease to exist. This brain shut-off mechanism was adaptive during prehistoric times. When primitive man was on the hunt, face-to-face with a ferocious predator, his mind was unavailable to analyze all the dangers—which was an advantage. "Is this tiger meat worth dying for? What if I fail? If I die, I'll never get laid again...Maybe, after all, I don't need the meat. The Caveman Chronicle just ran an article about the health benefits of a vegetarian diet. I think I'll try a tofu burger tonight instead." Before he could finish pondering these thought, he would have been hamburger meat in the beast's belly. During prehistoric times, cognitive shutdown was vital, not only for male's survival, but for the survival of the species as well.

Although the brain shutoff mechanism may have been a survival tool during a brief period in history, today that same mechanism may get a man "killed." When a furious woman comes at her man, the last thing he needs is a brain that's out to lunch. He needs all his higher order cognitive functions (e.g. reasoning, problem-solving skills) to handle this threat. Unfortunately, the precise tools that he needs to solve the conflict have just clicked-off, and he is completely unavailable for any productive exchange. This explains why there is a great deal of patterning to the fights that occur in chronically conflicted relationships. The fights always play out in the same way, because no creative thinking is available to explore alternate fighting tactics.

Another cause of the chronicity of marital conflicts is that it takes a man a long time-much longer than for a woman-for his internal chemistry to normalize following a stress. In fact, L. J. P. Van Doornen's research has shown that in relationships in which conflict is frequent, a man's chemistry never returns to baseline. With each subsequent fight, his arousal mounts higher and higher and his fuse becomes shorter and shorter, placing him at risk of acting out physically before he has a chance to flee. This risk is especially great for impulsive men who are already prone to physical acting out. It should be noted here that domestic violence is not the focus of this book. And if a woman is involved with a man who batters, or if she feels physically endangered, she is advised to seek professional help.

The point to keep in mind is that in all chronically conflicted relationships, residual ANS arousal and chronic cognitive shutdown fuel ongoing discord.

George returned home and, without his knowing it, a common fight was brewing.

"Did you buy the milk?" his wife Mary asked.

"No. I forgot," he answered, blank-faced.

"I reminded you to stop on your way home!" Mary sighed.

George stared at Mary, speechless.

"You aren't hearing a word I'm saying!"

"Yes I am!"

"What did I say?"

George stared at her, his jaw clenched.

"I'll refresh your memory. You said you forgot to get the milk!"

"I know!"

"So. What about the six-pack you're carrying?"

"Well...I bought it at the gas station," George said, closing his eyes.

"Since when did they stop selling milk at the gas station?"

"I can't remember everything. You don't care how hard my day was." He turned away.

"What's that got to do with the milk? As always you forgot, because what I want isn't important."

"That's not true, I buy you things," he said, still looking away.

"What?" Mary asked, raising her voice.

"Well, cookies, ice cream, pizza," he shouted.

"And...you eat them yourself. I'm tired of listening to your excuses. Admit it...you forgot the friggin' milk?"

"Yes, I forgot your freakin' milk. I have other more important things to think about, like how to survive life with a witch." George stormed out and slammed the door.

In the above example, George demonstrates a fatal case of brain meltdown due to chronic ANS arousal. Cognitive shutdown also caused George's inability to process communications, signaled by closing the eyes and looking away. Apart from becoming a mental midget, what else is happening to poor George? The muscles throughout his body are rigid, hence that blank, frozen stare that his wife interprets as his not caring about her. And, his muscles are tensed in preparation for fight or flight. Since George loves his wife, he does not want to fight her, so he flees instead.

The first form of fleeing George engaged in was psychic withdrawal. His mind escaped the scene; he tuned out, appeared deaf, and avoided eye contact. Mary became outraged by his seeming lack of caring and she cranked up the heat. George's ANS arousal mounted, and he slipped into verbal fleeing—hurling excuses, being defensive, denying, and refusing to accept responsibility for his upsetting behavior. The verbal fleeing further infuriated Mary ("How dare he turn the tables on me?") and she became more aggressive, which intensified George's ANS arousal.

Since verbal fleeing didn't succeed in defusing the situation, George's body physically fled. He escaped from the room in order to reestablish his chemical equilibrium; but, unfortunately, every time George physically withdraws, Mary interprets his behavior as further proof of his lack of caring. She becomes angrier and angrier; George's ANS arousal mounts higher and higher, so that he is constantly receiving internal signals to flee from danger. And, what's worse, these distress signals become part of his "normal" state of functioning. Constant ANS arousal causes chronic cognitive shutdown, which explains why George habitually forgets the milk. So long as George's chemistry remains disturbed, he will continue to withdraw. Mary, in turn, will continue to be angry, which insures the continuance of George's disturbed chemistry and their chronic fighting is the result.

Is Disturbed Body Chemistry (ANS Arousal) Causing Your Fighting?
A True-False Test for Women.

Our fights seem scripted. Our words, gestures, or actions rarely vary.	T or F
I can predict the outcome of our fights ahead of time.	T or F
When we fight, he seems to be frozen like a statue.	T or F
If I were to take his pulse, it would be racing (100 bpm or greater) during a fight.	T or F
My partner sweats during a fight.	T or F
My partner's muscles are very tight during a fight.	T or F
My partner turns away from me during a fight.	T or F
My partner closes his eyes and won't make eye contact with me during a fight.	T or F
My partner has a blank, frozen stare during a fight.	T or F
My partner defends, justifies, or counterblames during a fight.	T or F
My partner doesn't seem to be listening to me during a fight.	T or F
My partner physically leaves to escape a fight in progress.	T or F

15

My partner avoids me when he thinks a fight is brewing.	T or F

If you answered true to any of the above, we have a fairly clear idea that your partner's withdrawal and your chronic fights are caused by disturbed body chemistry. Why am I bothering to give you a chemistry lesson? Because, the first step to preventing the number one cause of relationship conflict and divorce starts with understanding that your husband's, lover's, or boyfriend's various withdrawal behaviors are not a sign of lack of love. They spring from a primitive, biologically based mechanism that he cannot help.

If this is the way men are wired, what can be done about it? Read on. In the following chapters, I will outline all the factors that heat the marital climate and discuss how to modify them. Until the thermostat is turned down, no conflict resolution can occur.

2

The Relationship Battleground: Rate Your Conflicts on the Fighting Richter Scale

Sue and Henry are standing in the bathroom embroiled in what might be called a plumbing power struggle. In the middle of the night, Henry always leaves the toilet seat up. Sue invariably falls in the bowl and receives an unwanted buttocks bath. Standing in the bathroom, her butt dripping wet, she began to wonder if another living soul could identify with the heartbreak of chapped cheeks.

If Sue had access to a library database, she could have researched the question. And, perhaps more importantly, she could determine if a judge would consider dishpan buns as grounds for divorce. Strange as it may seem, but many divorces have occurred over such seemingly trivial conflicts.

In this chapter, I will be discussing relationship conflict: The most common subjects of conflict and what causes conflict to turn into all-out fighting; and I will help you figure out whether you are suffering from out-of-control relationship warfare.

Before we go further, however, let's make sure you are clear on what constitutes conflict. It is a clash that occurs whenever opposing needs, wishes, goals, or opinions arise in a relationship. Since marriage and other intimate relationships are made up of two separate individuals, conflict and the angry feelings that go with it are normal and to be expected, according to researcher S. Duck, 1988.

What are the most common subjects of conflict? As you read over the following list, keep in mind that it is simply a quick overview and by no means definitive. You also need to know that complaints are generally issued by women-hence the fact that the complainer in the following examples is usually female.

Affection Conflicts

Disagreement over the frequency of affection displays (hugging, kissing, saying kind words, not enough romance, etc.). One spouse desires more emotional displays than the other is willing to give.

"The last time you kissed me was when we said, 'I do'!"

"You pet that dog more than me!"

"Do you think it would kill you to say something nice to me once before I die?"

"You're as romantic as a stuffed doll!"

Where's the Beef?
Otherwise Known as Sexual Conflicts

Conflicts over manner, frequency, technique, etc. The "when," "where," "how," "how much," "how long" (no, I'm not referring to measurements, although that could be a source of conflict as well) arguments.

"You're about as gentle as a buzz saw!"

"You think you might get in the mood before the century ends?"

Intimacy Issues

Disagreements regarding the degree of emotional and/or physical closeness/distance in the relationship. One partner wants more time apart than the other. One person never listens to the other's feelings or spends too little time at home and/or with the kids. One partner never communicates his/her own inner feelings to the other.

> *"You're always out with your friends or working!"*
> *"You never spend any time with me and the kids!"*

Leisure Arguments

Disagreements over how much time should be spent on leisure activities. Disagreements over what type of activities should be performed and whether these pursuits should be conducted separately or together.

> *"My idea of a good Sunday is not refilling beer pitchers for you and your friends!"*
> *"Do you think that we could do something together for a change?"*

Jealousy Fights

Whenever one partner pays attention to someone else, the other becomes insanely jealous. The jealous partner often thinks that the other is flirting with someone else (even when this is not true).

> *"Maybe you'd rather go home with her (or him)?"*

"Why didn't you announce to everyone that you had the hots for him (or her)?"

"I saw you holding her shoulder and caressing her neck!"

"You said you would be in your office until seven. I called you at six thirty. There was no answer. Where were you?"

Household Chore Arguments

Disagreements over the perceived lack of fairness in the division of chores arising from one partner's feeling stuck with a disproportionate share of the responsibilities or from one partner's refusal to assist around the house.

"Where is it written that I'm the only one who should wash the dishes (or
    do the laundry, etc.)?"

"How many times do I have to tell you to pick up your papers from the friggin' counter?"

Lack-of -Follow-Through Arguments

In these arguments, it is generally the woman who is angry at her partner for not following through with his agreed upon tasks.

"You forgot to take the garbage out, AGAIN!"

"It was your turn to pick up Johnny from soccer. Where were you?"

Lack-of-Initiative Arguments

With these type of arguments, one partner is angry that the other doesn't even notice, or seem to care, that various tasks require attention.

"How many months are you going to wait before fixing the broken kitchen window?"

"When were you going to notice that Sally's bike has had a flat tire for four months?"

Parenting Arguments

Disagreement over the degree of lenience/strictness; feeling that one partner undermines the other, doesn't enforce the rules that have been agreed upon, or reverses the decisions of the other parent. Feelings of resentment over unequal distribution of child-care responsibilities.

"You're like one of the kids. You let them do whatever they want!"

"What are you, an army sergeant?"

"Why should I bother making rules, when you just let the kids break them?"

"This fabric that I'm holding in my hand is called a diaper. Do you think it would kill you to change one every now and then?"

In-Law Arguments

Fights over loyalty issues, such as feeling sided against in a family argument. Disagreements on how much time should be spent with the in-laws.

"Why don't you marry your mother?"
"You always take their side over mine!"
"Since you want to see your folks so much, why don't we just move in with them!"

Friendship Arguments

Disagreements over choice of friends; how much time should be spent socializing with friends in the absence of the partner spouse; how much time should be spent socializing with friends or other couples.

"Why did you marry me? You obviously like being with your buddies more than me!"

"I don't like your friend, Walter. He always puts me down. Why do we have to spend time with him?"

Value Conflicts

Disagreements over life goals; what is important in life; cultural, religious, or sexual values; drinking and/or smoking habits; not seeing eye to eye on tastes or interests, which includes conflicts over what is proper behavior in social situations.

"Now I know why you call your Land Rover a pickup truck! And, no, I'm not interested in turning your backseat into my box spring."

"You make Ben Franklin look like a big spender!"

"You shouldn't drink on Sunday!"

"You don't go to church enough!"

"Why do we need to redecorate so often?"

Selfishness or Lack-of-Cooperation Arguments

An unwillingness to work with the partner toward a mutually satisfying resolution of whatever the conflict is. One partner feels that the other is persistently stubborn or unresponsive.

> *"You don't give a damn how I feel!"*
> *"You don't care about what I want!"*

Control Freak Arguments

In these arguments, one of the partners feels controlled or manipulated by the other. A partner or spouse who needs to be in control is often frightened of being controlled. Thus, the person who rules others does so in order to prevent him- or herself from being taken over.

> *"Why does it always have to be your way?"*
> *"You're not my father."*

Money Arguments

Disagreements over bills, how much money should be allocated to savings versus how much should be spent outright. Disagreements over one partner's overspending, stinginess, or overly controlling stance with regard to money.

> *"You're as tight as a frog's butt!"*
> *"You spend money like water!"*
> *"There's always money to buy your computer, your printer, your software programs, even your computer games. For me, it's never in the budget. I haven't bought a dress in the last three years."*

Power Struggle Arguments

The partners struggle over any issue that you can imagine and neither is willing to yield. There are no compromises, and the mates soon feel like dogs fighting over the same bone. The movie, *The War of the Roses*, depicts a power struggle that ends in death. Remember, that even if one partner succeeds in prevailing, both partners are losers when power struggles have taken over the relationship.

> *"You always need to have it your way!"*
> *"I'd die before I'd give in to you."*

You're-Shutting-Me-Out Arguments

In these types of arguments, it is usually the woman who complains that her partner doesn't disclose himself to her.

> *"You never let me in."*
> *"I know something is bothering you. Why won't you talk to me?"*

You-Never-Listen-to-Me Arguments

The You-Never-Listen-to-Me argument is a common relationship beef. And, once again, it is the woman who usually complains about not being emotionally heard.

> *"Why can't you just listen to what I'm saying?"*
> *"Don't walk away from me when I'm talking."*

Whatever you are chronically fighting about probably

fits into one of the above categories. Interestingly, these sources of conflict are not only remarkably consistent from nation to nation, but, with the exception of the You-Never-Listen-to-Me argument, they occur among happy couples as well. So, you ask, why are they happy and why am I so unhappy? The reason is simple. Studies have shown that while happy couples fight about exactly the same things that unhappy couples do, happy couples do not fight *habitually* on these subjects. They have acquired the interactional tools that permit them to resolve their conflicts, whereas unhappy couples employ ineffective conflict resolution techniques so that their disagreements cycle out of control long before they can ever reach the resolution stage. That is, their fighting becomes so heated that the man withdraws and no resolution occurs. In the next chapter, I will help you identify the various behaviors that are causing your conflicts to cycle out of control. And, in later chapters, I will show you how to apply more effective techniques so that you can pull in the reins long before your conflicts become run-away horses.

Conflict versus Fighting

It is necessary to make the distinction between conflict and fighting. The words are often used interchangeably, despite the fact that they are different. Whenever one's needs and wishes are thwarted a state of conflict results. If the conflict is not resolved amicably, anger arises. It is how one handles the anger that determines whether or not a conflict will become a fight.

Most unhappy couples do not know how to channel angry feelings into constructive communications. Instead, they think that angry feelings are synonymous with angry actions; and they "act out" their anger. The distinction between the feeling of anger and the "acting out" of anger is essential because anger is a neutral emotion, a warning light that your psychological toes have been stepped on. The acting out of anger through hostile behavior (door slamming, shoving, etc.) or hostile words (name- calling, sarcasm, threats and insults) is a big problem. Hostile words and actions evolve into fighting. You may say to me, "My relationship problems are driving me crazy and if I couldn't blow off steam, I'd lose it for sure." While you may feel better at the moment you drop your load, what you probably don't realize is that the ranting, raving, screaming, yelling and slamming actually causes more problems.

There was an era when therapists touted the benefits of emotional "venting." A branch of psychology, known as the cathartic school, propounded the notion that it is healthy to scream and yell in order to reach to the bottom of one's emotional barrel; kind of like an enema for the soul. This approach to handling emotions has been largely abandoned because, as it turns out, anger has a self-feeding aspect—anger begets more anger. In addition, emotional venting has a negative effect on the partner who is being dumped on. I have already explained in chapter one why acting out of intense emotions triggers a chemical reaction in men that actually causes more marital conflict. But, for now let's just focus on the point that raw emotion should never be dumped on a mate; that is, not if you want to resolve your conflicts and achieve relationship harmony.

If acting out anger doesn't work, what about expressing angry feelings in words? Now, I'm really going to throw you a curve ball by saying that angry feelings should never be "expressed." What I mean is that the raw, angry emotions should never be delivered in pure form to your mate. I find it helpful to use the image of a sieve when talking about intense, angry emotions. Before discussing with your mate what is bothering you, your raw emotions need to be filtered through this imaginary sieve. What remains in the sieve is to be kept for yourself, and only what passes through the sieve of your intellect is fit for human consumption. The important point here is that once the emotions have passed through this sieve they have been transformed and detoxified.

Roger is a thirty year old copy editor in a daily newspaper. He chain smokes, while ranting about the lousy copy reporters turn in, and at home, he rules his family with an iron fist. When his kids stray from what he has decided is the right path, he barrages them with fits of rage. And, if his wife Jane, a sexy, bleached blond, dares to smile at another man during a party, she receives a verbal lashing during the ride home. After years of suffering these unbearable explosions, Jane bore her soul to her minister, who referred her to me.

I met with Roger, who explained that his wife and kids made him so furious that he could not control his behavior—the mesh of his emotional sieve was as widely spaced as the San Andreas Fault. I inquired about other situations in which Roger expressed powerful rage.

"What about your boss? Doesn't he make you angry at times?" I asked.

"Yeah, he pisses me off all the time," Roger admitted.

"And, how many times have you given it to him?" Roger blinked a couple of times, obviously thinking, this shrink I got is really off her rocker. "Yell at him? Are you nuts, Doc.? I need my job. You think I'm crazy!"

So, Roger had the ability to control himself, when he wanted to. He had an emotional sieve with a very fine mesh at his disposal. That is, when Roger realizes that his opponent has more power than he does—the power to fire him, as in the case of his boss—then he can be a good boy.

"If you are able to control your behavior when you are enraged at a boss that you hate, then you can control yourself when dealing with your wife and kids that you love." I said.

Roger was speechless. I advised him to join one of my therapy groups for impulsive behavior. After a few months of regular attendance, Roger had decided to use, with his wife and kids, the same sieve that had proven so effective in filtering his emotions when his boss enraged him. He had put his emotions under his control.

It is essential that you learn to harness your raw emotions and transform them into constructive communications that are helpful to you, your mate, and your relationship. The key here is this: how anger is handled makes or breaks a relationship. Remember as you read on, it is acted out anger that causes occasional relationships conflicts to turn into out-of-control fighting.

Fight Habituation

For some couples, out-of-control fighting is precisely what they unconsciously want to maintain. No matter how uncomfortable their fighting may be, the prospect of not fighting may be even more uncomfortable. For example, chronic fighting may ward off other feelings that may be too terrifying to one or both of the mates. Being hooked on fighting is what psychologists call fight habituation.

Mark and Joan are a classic example of what I call Fighting Junkies. Mark is terrified of intimacy and whenever they seem to be getting along better, he does something to make Joan angry. He gets a speeding ticket, which depletes their savings, and the fighting that ensues serves to keep Joan at a comfortable distance. No matter how hard they try to change, they always end up fighting again.

As with any addiction, trying to kick the habit can make you feel sicker before you feel better. How can you tell if you're hooked on fighting? Take this simple test.

Are You a Fighting Junkie?

I secretly look for things to fight about.	T or F
I feel most comfortable when at war.	T or F
I go for the kill when we're fighting, saying and doing things that I know will push my mate's buttons.	T or F
I don't want to let my partner close to me; I'm afraid he would hurt or reject me.	T or F
My mother and father used to fight all the time when I was a kid.	T or F
We have been fighting ever since our relationship began, even when we were dating..	T or F

If you answered yes to any of the above questions, you may be a Fighting Junkie and you will need to pay extra attention to chapter five, Battle Scars, which will help you get beyond your addiction.

Out-of-control fighting is not always caused by an unconscious need to ward off closeness. It may also result from a deficit in conflict resolution skills. Without these skills, fighting becomes a runaway horse; and once it's taken off, the horse is very hard to get back in the stable. There is more. What is true of one single fighting episode is true also of the life sequence of relationship fights. Multiple, unresolved conflicts follow a downward spiral that is not unlike chronic illness. Left untreated, a physical illness usually worsens; whereas, if you catch the illness early enough, and intervene properly, you are likely to cure the problem. The same is true for an intimate relationship. It is a living, breathing entity and if you abuse it and ignore its signs of sickness, it will die.

The first step towards a cure and to gaining control—is to determine the severity of your fighting.

Rate Your Conflicts on the Fighting Richter Scale

In the following pages, rate your fights on my Fighting Richter Scale. The stages below are the three main gradations on the scale, Stage Three being the most advanced.

Stage One—The Broken Record

The first sign that fighting is out of control is technically referred to as *Stability of Conflict,* or what I call the Broken Record phenomenon. Do you find yourself bringing up the same issues over and over again? No matter how trivial the subjects of conflict may seem, if you are regularly conflicting on the same issues, you're in big trouble. What does the Broken Record phenomenon look like?

> *"I hate it when you walk around the house in your bra and panties—with the shades open. How many*

times have I asked you not to do it? 100, 200, 500 times? Each time you say O.K., but two days later you do it again. Here's the phone, why don't you just call the neighbor and tell him you're ready to sleep with him?"

♡

"This morning, for the six hundredth time, you didn't put the cap on the toothpaste tube. I'm fed up with you!"

♡

"I have asked you to avoid making day time phone calls to your mother in Florida. I asked you last year, last month, last week and even two days ago. But you do it again and again. Why don't you move to Florida with her?"

If you find yourself arguing recycled issues, no doubt about it, you are stuck in Stage One. You need to learn the conflict resolution skills presented in this book, or you will soon slip into Stage Two.

Stage Two—Male Withdrawal

Stage Two emerges when your areas of conflict have become major hot spots. This Stage is like the old French proverb, Cats that have been burned by hot water become afraid of cold water. In other words, all you have to do is bring up the recycled issue and your partner's fur is already bristling.

Marjorie's husband goes bowling too many nights a week. For months she complained more and more about it, while he sat there listening to her tirades.

31

*Eventually, he turned a deaf ear, and now, all she has
to do is open her mouth to speak, and the bowling ball
is in his hand and he's rolling out the door.*

In Stage Two, a man has begun to withdraw physically, emotionally, or psychically whenever a conflict discussion arises or whenever he thinks one is brewing. The following list gives you, in more detail than in the previous chapter, the classic signs of male withdrawal.

✓ When you try to talk to your partner about what's bothering you, he stares off into space, and has a blank expression.

✓ He turns away from you, or avoids eye contact when you try to speak.

✓ He becomes sullen and silent and appears not to be listening.

✓ He defends himself in words, hurls all kinds of excuses, and denies whatever is the issue on the table. Or, he tries to counterattack by telling you what you have done wrong since day one.

✓ He physically leaves the room or the house.

✓ He spends as much time as possible away from home, or hides out in his study, his workshop, or disappears by watching television for hours.

If you find that your partner is exhibiting any of the above behaviors, you are locked in the Demand/Withdraw

Negative Escalation Cycle, and, according to J. M. Gottman and N. Silver, if you don't apply the principles in my book (and pay particular attention to cooling down the relationship climate), statistics show that you will likely be separated or divorced within three years.

Stage Three—The Bitter End

In this stage you are so tired of fighting that you have begun to give up. You may have stopped bringing up the troublesome issues because you are in the process of detaching psychologically. Maybe you are fantasizing about having an affair or you are making plans for your future, and the plans don't include your partner. This is a process that is similar to coming to terms with the death of a loved one. First there is anger, then there is detachment and, finally, acceptance. In this stage you are trying to convince yourself that you don't care anymore, so that the leaving won't be so painful. When relationship distress has reached this level, if you are asked to remember the good times you have shared as a couple, your memory will draw a blank. It's as if your mind has pulled its own plug so that your heart won't suffer too much when you dissolve the relationship.

Ben and Josephine have been together for fourteen years. He owns an auto repair shop. She is a hair-dresser. Josephine has often asked Ben to tell her when he would be back home. She begged him, she cried, she screamed. He continued to come home when he pleased, often at 10 o'clock, only to throw himself in bed, snoring even before his head hit the pillow.

"Hi, how are you?" he mumbled, stumbling, half-drunk, into the bedroom.

"O.K.," she called from the bathroom, while pre-paring to meet her friend at the local hangout. She put on her coat and walked to the front door. "Good night," she said flatly, before closing the door.

If Ben and Josephine do not apply my techniques quickly, they will soon become a divorce statistic Even if you, too, are in Stage Three, don't despair. The techniques that you will soon learn have helped other desperate couples, even those on the verge of signing divorce papers, rekindle the love they thought was long lost. But, before you can resolve the conflicts that have transformed your relationship into a cold war, your hearts must thaw.

If you are suffering from chronic fighting, and find yourself caught in any of the three stages mentioned above, the next thing you must do is identify and eradicate the Fight Traps and faulty conflict resolution tactics that stand between you and relationship harmony.

3

The No Fly (off the Handle) Zone: Eliminating Fight Traps and Faulty Conflict Resolution Tactics

Each of the Fight Traps and faulty conflict resolution tactics discussed in this chapter throws oil on the fire and keeps couples stuck on the fighting treadmill. If you want to achieve relationship harmony, you must lose them all. Before we get down to identifying your Fight Traps and faulty conflict resolution tactics, we first need to find out if you are truly ready to give them up.

Every night after work, Fred practices the same ritual without deviation. He deposits his shoes at the back door, nestles into his favorite easy chair, pours himself a scotch, browses through the paper, and dozes.

We humanoids are creatures of habit and there is a permanent tug of war going on inside all of us: On one level we want to move ahead and on another we want to stay the same. Take the following test.

If I am honest with myself, I'd have to admit that I'd feel like a fish out of water without our chronic fights gnawing at the guts of our relationship. *Yes or No.*

I am afraid that we wouldn't know how to relate to each other if we stopped our fighting. *Yes or No.*

I am afraid that if we let go of our fighting, another worse problem would appear. *Yes or No.*

I am afraid that if I allow myself to believe things can change for the better, that I will be terribly disappointed if this doesn't happen. *Yes or No.*

If you said yes to the first or second statement you are suffering from fear of the unknown. It is a normal fear.

Each night, Jennifer makes sure that Joseph's dinner is ready at 6:30. Joseph, who is an accountant, told her that he'd be arriving later and later each night as the tax deadline approached. When this started happening, Jennifer was convinced that he was using the taxes as a pretext for avoiding her. And, when he finally arrived home, she lashed out at him. He silently tolerated this verbal lashing—eventually she'd run out of gas and there would be peace until the next time. For him, being yelled at was part of marriage—his mother always screamed at his father. At least there were no surprises.

One day, Jennifer complained to her friend Susan about her problem with Joseph. Susan, whose father was also an accountant, told Jennifer that her father stayed out till 11 p.m. during tax season. Jennifer realized that she was misinterpreting Joseph's lateness.

When he returned home that night, she did not scream at him, but welcomed him with a kiss and a big hello. Joseph felt frightened. What's going on? Has Jennifer poisoned my stew? What does she want from me? Maybe she's horny and wants to force me into hav-

*ing sex....Not another hour and half to stay awake...and
on a night when I'm so tired. Joseph began sweating.
His guts were in a knot. He had become so accustomed
to their nightly fight that he hardly knew how to live
without it. He is suffering from fear of the unknown.*

True, the unknown can be scary. But, chronic fighting
is even more scary. What do you risk by staying with the familiar? These risks include physical violence, illness, depression,
infidelity, and divorce. Write down all the risks you face from
staying the same.

As you ponder all the terrible risks associated with
staying stuck on the fighting treadmill, aren't you more willing
to risk the new?

What about the last two statements, "If we let go of
our fighting, another, worse problem will appear" and "If I
allow myself to believe that things can change for the better, I
will be terribly disappointed when this doesn't happen." Both
fears express a defeatist attitude. It's like saying, "I know I'm
doomed, so why try for better?" This hopeless feeling may be
coming from the fact that you haven't been able to make head-
way on your relationship problems. It's normal to feel defeated
when things aren't going well. But, after reading this book you
will have proven techniques to use to combat this attitude.

There is also a deeper meaning behind this defeatist
attitude. Your mind is using this hopeless philosophy as a
protection against feeling hurt or disappointed. If you try and
fail, of course you would feel let down. So, in order to protect yourself, your mind has convinced you not to try. ("Why
bother trying, it won't work anyway.") True, if you don't
expend effort in trying to change the situation, then you don't
have to risk failure, hurt or disappointment. But, the irony is
that, by not trying, you are failing yourself and your relation-

ship. Remember, the only real failures are those who don't try. Identifying the fears that keep you clinging to the familiar is the first step toward resolving them. I also suggest that you frequently reread the three paragraphs above, which will help to further soften your fears. When your fears no longer have you by the throat, you are ready to move on to the next step: to identify and eliminate the Fight Traps that are holding your relationship hostage.

In the last twenty plus years, I have worked with many couples, from all walks of life, and this work has yielded a fascinating finding: Fight Traps cut across state lines, class lines, power lines, age lines and any other kind of lines you can think of. That is to say, all conflicted couples engage in them.

When I conducted research for this book, I searched the literature and was surprised that I could not find a comprehensive list of Fight Traps. So what you are about to read is the first exhaustive list, which I have broken down into two categories: Open Warfare and Secret Warfare.

It is important that you realize that every trap is faulty. I am stressing this point because most of us engage in behaviors that are so natural that they seem like a second skin. No matter how "normal" these Fight Traps may seem to you, remember that they are neither "normal" nor healthy. Each and every one of them maintains and escalates relationship conflict and keeps you stuck in a permanent state of war. So, if you are committed to achieving marital harmony, it would be wise to identify the Fight Traps you and your mate use and trash them.

Fight Traps: Open Warfare

Counterblaming
In distressed relationships, couples rarely listen to each other and will miss no opportunity to throw the blame back on

each other. Counterblaming escalates conflict and precludes resolution.

> Mary: "I asked you not to leave your underwear beside the bed."
> Pete: "I told you not to hang your stockings in the shower."
> Mary: "You always have an answer. Mr. Perfect."
> Pete: "You're the one who's answering back."

Verbal Attacking

As you will see in the following example, Verbal Attacking leads to defensive responses and verbal counterattacks.

> Marie is standing in the laundry room, the blue vein at her temple beating faster than a rap tune. As Josh enters the room, she hurls a wet towel at his head, and it coils like a sheik's turban, around his skull.
> "You seem to be clueless to the fact that laundry needs to be done each week," she snarls.
> "Oh, like I do nothing around the house (defensive). Not that you would notice (counterattack)," he shouts, peeling the towel from his head.

Score Keeping

Couples get caught in score keeping to boost their eroding egos, and we'll talk about this in greater depth in chapter 6. For now, I simply want to show you how to recognize score keeping and it's variants. Keep in mind that once a couple resorts to score keeping, they will use any ammunition necessary in order to win. Consequently, it is not unusual to find that all the tactics described in this section may be creatively combined in order to strengthen the punch.

Mike: This is the fifth time that I told you to fold my socks flat and not in a ball.

Sue: Well, as long as we're counting, it's been a hundred times that I told you to stop piling your junk mail on your night table.

Mike: If you're gonna try to paint me as the pig, I think you better look at your closet, it's got a thousand pieces of junk thrown in there!

Sue: Since you're so good with numbers, here's the phone. Dial your mother's number and tell her you're moving back in with her.

Winners/Losers

Elaine: You forgot to pick up my car part.

Rick: I'm sorry.

Elaine: I can't rely on you.

Rick: I said I was sorry. You won't be satisfied until you grind me into the dirt.

Elaine: That's where you belong!

I'm Right/You're Wrong

Fred: You shouldn't face the net when you're hitting a backhand shot.

Sarah: I'm married to Jimmy friggin' Conners!

Fred: I'm just telling you how to improve your shot. You know that I am a better player than you.

Sarah: Yes, you're right. You're a better player and a better chef and a better expert in everything.

Fred: What are you talking about? I never pretended to be a laundry expert!

40

Character Assassination
Name-calling. Insults. Put-downs

Steve: You know you are a real loser!
Louise: You should talk. You're lazy as hell!
Steve: I'm not the gutless one who won't dare ask for a raise.

Globalizing
"You always"/"You never"

Brenda: You know you never take me on dates anymore.
Scott: You're always nagging me, why would I want to?

Kitchen Sinking
Throwing everything that's bothering either mate into one discussion.

Rose: I'm pretty fed up with your falling asleep on the couch.
Rich: I'm tired.
Rose: You're tired; you never have time to spend with the kids. You never talk to me anymore. There's no romance.
Rich: Anything else.
Rose: Yeah, and you don't make enough money.

Throwing Oil on the Fire
When couples use this Fight Trap, they make inflammatory

comments that they know will anger the other. This Trap is popularly referred to as pushing someone's buttons.

> *Suzie: I have a good mind to call my old boyfriend and ask him to take me out.*
> *Robert: You know how it drives me crazy when you get back at me by trying to make me jealous.*

Fighting Dirty or Hitting Below the Belt

In this Fight Trap, the angry person will use out-of-context information to deliver a low blow. For example, let's say a wife reveals to her mate that she is upset because her boss said that her work isn't well organized. Then, a few days later, she tells her mate that he's being too messy around the house. The hitting-below-the-belt fighter would get even with his wife by saying something like, "Who are you to talk? I thought you won the Miss Piggy award at the office."

Ancient History

When someone brings up something that the other said or did in the recent or remote past, I call this the Ancient History Fight Trap.

> *Emily: Here we go again. You're looking at that woman with lust. Just like you did with the blond last week.*
> *Eric: I am not.*
> *Emily: You sure are. You've been doing this since the first day of our marriage....Remember when we were sitting at the bar on our honeymoon...?*

Exploding

When angered, the exploder goes out of control—screams, rants, raves, and may even become verbally or physically abusive. This behavior has two effects on the receiving partner: he or she either becomes a doormat or attacks back. In the latter case, physical violence often results. Professional help is needed when explosive behavior is present.

Me Big Chief, You Little Indian: Power Plays

This tactic is used by a person who possesses power over his/her partner. Power can be in the form of money, or better looks, or even the knowledge that the other partner is so in love with or dependent that he/she would put up with garbage rather than risk losing the relationship. When someone misuses power, he or she is the boss and there is no discussion or collaboration. The big chief is usually quite happy with this approach, because he gets what he wants. But he'd better watch out: The little Indian is probably doing a slow burn, and one day the chief may find his scalp—or worse—cut off.

I said our daughter is not going on that trip and that's the end of the discussion.

or

This discussion is terminated.

or

My answer is final.

One-Upmanship

Bob: You think you've got something to cry about. I've got more stress on me in an ordinary day of work than you have in a month.

Bridgette: Poor you. You've got it so tough. Who do

you think got up last night to take care of Suzy?

Recruiting Allies
Getting outsiders or family members to take sides.

> Sharon: *My mother even told me that you're wrong not*
> *to pay for my new dress.*
> Tom: *Why doesn't she pay for it?*
> Sharon: *She's not my husband. She said that if you*
> *were a good husband, you'd pay for it.*
> Tom: *The guys at work think that I should buy a cheaper*
> *wife!*

Fight Traps: Secret Warfare

In Secret Warfare, partners still escalate conflicts; they just do so in subtler, less overt ways. Keep in mind that secret warfare still fuels ongoing fighting.

Guilt Trip
I hope you're satisfied; you got me so upset over your temper outburst that I have a terrible headache.

Silent Treatment
> Steve: *How long are you going to ignore me?*
> Marie: *Walks away, as though deaf.*

Withholding
In order to express his or her anger, the withholder, consciously or unconsciously, doesn't provide whatever it is the other person wants.

44

I get it. No sex for me until I buy you flowers.

or

Ethel: Did you remember we have a date tonight?

Scott: I just forgot.

Ethel: You always "forget" when I made you mad the night before!

Silent Sabotage

This Fight Trap is a combination of silent treatment and withholding. The person doesn't verbally express anger, but rather gets even silently or indirectly.

Monty: You keep burning my dinner.

Gabrielle: I don't know what you mean.

Monty: You've been mad at me all week. You burned dinner three times and you also wrecked three of my shirts.

I Told You So

Karl: The toilet's broken again!

Betty: I told you not to use that plumber. You should have listened to me!

Sarcasm

In distressed relationships, sarcasm often takes the form of a statement that communicates agreement that isn't truly meant.

Bud: Yes, you're right (smirking).

Natalie: Don't "yes me." You know you don't mean it.

Bud: Oh, but I do mean it. Every husband wants his wife to take a twenty-five-thousand-dollar trip across the

45

globe with her sisters.

Ambusher

The ambusher is a person who hides in the bushes, waiting to launch a surprise attack or to prey upon the spouse when he or she is weakest.

I can't believe you choose this moment—when I'm upset—to complain about my lovemaking techniques.

Indirect Digs

In this trap, one partner doesn't directly tell the other what he or she is angry about, but waits until they are in public, then drops snide remarks. For example, Sue and Mike are out to dinner with friends. The night before, Mike rushed foreplay and she didn't say anything at the time. As the group waits for their table, Sue's friend says, "I'm so hungry I can hardly wait." To which Sue replies, in a loud voice, "You're not the only one. My husband can't wait either."

Nagging, Whining, and Complaining: The Three Scrooges

Women are particularly inclined to express anger indirectly by resorting to these three self-explanatory behaviors. They are particularly dangerous Fight Traps because they always provoke husband withdrawal.

Faulty Conflict Resolution Tactics

Now that we have discussed the various Fight Traps, let's identify a few more potholes on the path to relationship harmony. Conflict resolution impasses can be due to universal obstacles; couple type; and individual obstacles—the faulty conflict resolution tactics of one or both partners.

The primary universal obstacle to resolution is ANS arousal. So, when your partner seems unwilling to work with you, check his pulse or his pits; if his Safeguard has stopped working, you know ANS arousal has kicked in. And if ANS arousal is in full swing, you must wait to discuss matters. No man can sit for a conflict discussion until his arousal level has diminished. Other universal obstacles are listed in the following section.

Universal Obstacles to Conflict Resolution

Old Scars

Old Scars interfere with conflict resolution in two ways. First, when a woman's Old Scars are activated by her partner's behavior, she will become very emotionally upset, which will trigger ANS arousal in her partner. Likewise, a man's unresolved Old Scars are likely to interfere with his ability to negotiate with his partner. This, in turn, will anger her and trigger his ANS arousal. In chapter 5, I discuss Old Scars fully and I will help you determine whether they are fueling your fights and interfering with your negotiation potential. The point to remember now is this: you will need to provide each other with the necessary emotional healing as a precondition to resolving your conflicts.

The Seesaw Effect

If ANS arousal and Old Scars are not causing your mate's refusal to collaborate or negotiate, there's a good chance that the Seesaw Effect is operating. It is believed that when there is love, a man will move mountains to keep that love. But, no matter how much a man loves you, love and power are hinged together much like a seesaw. When power is on the upswing, the willingness to collaborate is often on the downswing. This leads to what I call the Male Power Play.

Male Power Play: Refusal to Negotiate

Many women are bereft of power in their relationships. They either don't earn as much as their spouses or don't earn at all. In many cases, women need their partners for survival and their partners know it. Unfortunately, this creates an imbalance of power that interferes with negotiating potential. Think in business terms. Whenever two or more parties come to the negotiation table, if they want the negotiation to be successful, that is, to bring satisfaction to both parties, they should possess equality of power or assets. Without equality, one party will invariably be crushed.

Many women describe feeling squashed during "negotiations." As Terrie told me, "He knows we need him and couldn't make it without him. When things get hot, he's quick to remind me where the door is." Unfortunately, many women live with the pain of their partners' misuse of power. You can be sure that power plays exist in your relationship when your mate directly or indirectly communicates that he doesn't need to change—you're stuck with him; or when you think, I have to put up with whatever he's doing, because I can't live without him. Betty Carter and J. K. Peter's book, *Love, Honor & Negotiate* describes the impact of inequality in marriage and details how to shift the scales of power.

Female Power Play: Manipulation

When men misuse their power, it is common for women to resort to the only power play they know: manipulation. Winning is still the unconscious goal, but it is expressed in a subtle, rather than overtly aggressive way. Various manipulation cards can be played alone or in conjunction: spending money to get even, refusal of sex, threats of abandonment, flirting with other men, withdrawal of love, and/or guilt trips. Everyone is familiar with these tactics. While they may "work" in the short run because a woman may receive what she wants, manipulation always backfire in the long run. This is because the person on the receiving end of the manipulation feels angry; and anger causes ANS arousal, defensiveness, and withdrawal. In short, no healthy negotiations can occur when a mate is defensive or simply gone.

Why would a woman resort to such ineffective tactics? Sometimes manipulation is all a woman knows.

Lucille's mother was a passive woman who tolerated a drunken, abusive husband. She could never directly address her husband regarding his behavior because of his miserable temper and because she needed his pay-check; instead, she resorted to various manipulations in an attempt to control his behavior. She hid his car keys or faked an illness so that he would be forced to stay home and care for her rather than go out drinking. Lucille learned from her mother that women manipulate in order to get what they want. Cut to twenty years later. When Lucille feels neglected, instead of saying directly that she wants attention, she complains that she has a sore shoulder from ironing his shirts, and hopes that he will feel guilty, drop his ball game, and pay attention to her. Unfortunately, her behavior only irritates him and sends him farther away.

Why else do women resort to manipulation rather than negotiation? Many women lack financial power, but what about sexual power? I'm sure you know women whose sexuality is a cannon aimed directly at their spouses. If the husband is "good," he gets it; if he isn't, it's a sexual diet of bread and water and self-service restaurants. When a woman uses sex as a power tool or weapon, it always backfires; and she soon becomes a victim of chronic relationship conflict. The point is, a woman must find a nonsexual way of equalizing the power in her relationship and until she does, no negotiations are possible.

> *Amelia felt crushed by her husband. He often stayed out with the boys and was deaf to her pleas and her rage when he returned home. It wasn't until she decided to increase her own power by starting a career that the marriage began to change. Merely beginning school was enough to upset the power applecart. Amelia didn't need to threaten divorce or engage in other relationship-destructive acts (like having an affair). She simply moved ahead with her life. This was all that was needed to communicate her message: I refuse to allow you to crush me. I will get on with my life with or without you. This wake-up call was quite effective because her husband realized that he loved her and didn't want to lose her. He began to improve his behavior and negotiate a more acceptable arrangement.*

Often making the decision that you are ready, willing, and able to move on is sufficient to ring your husband's wake-up bell. Making this simple mental shift causes the seesaw to switch position; suddenly your husband realizes how much he loves you and drops his muscle flexing.

Equalizing the power is one way to improve your bargaining power, but there still may be other obstacles to negotiation. These obstacles operate at the level of the couple.

Couple Type and Conflict Resolution Blocks

In her classic study, M. A. Fitzpatrick identified four basic couple types, Traditionals, Separates, Independents, and Mixed, and as you will see, each type is prone to its own unique brand of unhealthy conflict negotiations. Understanding your couple type, will offer clues to your negotiation roadblocks, and the structured negotiation techniques presented later in the book, will enable you to steer clear of these blocks.

Traditional couples are like Ozzie and Harriet. They have an old-fashioned approach to sex-roles and division of household tasks, and they tend to agree on marital and family concerns. Hence, Traditionals have the least amount of relationship conflict. However, conflict still exists. The traditional wife's tendency to overlook areas of conflict and swallow her feelings places her in danger of becoming depressed or developing psychosomatic illnesses that may include tension headaches, and stomach and bowel disturbances. Suppressed feelings may also result in periodic explosions of anger. For such wives, learning to become more direct regarding areas of conflict may become necessary, especially if they are showing signs of fraying around the emotional edges.

Separates are as the name sounds. They tend to be cut-off from their mates, spend much time apart, and disclose more of their true feelings to friends. According to research, Separates avoid direct conflict with their mates. It would appear that Separate couples maintain their distance so as not to spark the intense emotions that lurk beneath their veneer of indifference. If both partners are satisfied with this arrangement, no problem exists, at least in the short run. But, more often than not, one or both parties wake up—for example, when they meet someone whom they are attracted to—and realize that they have no relationship with their partner. In such cases, the relationship quickly dissolves. If Separates decide to brave the sea of emotional separation, and address their areas of conflict, they must be sure to first master all partial identification and listening techniques, discussed in chapters 7 and 8, before attempting any conflict resolution.

Independent couples are assertive in their communications and often find themselves caught in conflicts over big and small issues. There is little agreement on division of household tasks, displays of affection, and they often argue about whether or not to separate and divorce. On surveys, Independents see themselves as self-disclosing but see their partners as being unwilling to reveal themselves. These couples need to be aware of their tendency to negotiate on trivial matters and learn to distinguish big from small. In addition, since Independents engage in open displays of conflict, they must learn to cool down their communications, and, alternately, listen and self-disclose, activities that are all sorely lacking in the Independents' marriage.

Mixed couples can exhibit any or all of the above characteristics, and they should adopt the recommendations that apply to the couple type they most resemble.

Individual Obstacles

Conflict resolution blocks can also operate on an individual level. If you want to resolve your conflicts, you must identify and surrender the faulty conflict resolution tactics that you learned in your family of origin. The following is a list of the faulty tactics that many individuals employ.

Yielding

The person that yields (usually female) attempts to resolve conflicts by committing psychological suicide. She sweeps herself under the rug by surrendering even on issues that are greatly important to her. Reasons for yielding include: fear of confrontation, which often stems from feelings of dependency and powerlessness; fear of making her spouse angry; fear of abandonment; low self-esteem (wanting to be liked); or fear of saying or doing horrible things in anger. The yielder often rationalizes her feelings away by telling herself: "It's not important"; or "Peace is better than fighting"; or "God loves humble persons"; or "Who am I to impose my views?" or "I love him and must make concessions."

> *Husband: You are such a lousy cook. How many times do I have to tell you that Kitty Chow tastes better than your tuna casserole.*
> *Wife: I'm sorry dear, I'll throw the recipe away.*

It is common also for the yielder to put up with all sorts of abuses, and never address her own feelings of anger. She lives under the illusion that if she silently tolerates whatever garbage is heaped on her, her mate will eventually reward her patience. Instead of being rewarded, the doormat digs a deeper grave for herself; and, rather than earning appreciation and love, her tolerance trains her mate to continue abusing her. Meanwhile, the conflict goes unresolved.

Habitual Conflict Avoidance: The Ostrich Policy

This tactic is based on self-deception; fooling oneself into believing that if the problem is ignored, "it" will go away. For example, a husband comes home late, after having spent hours playing pool at a strip bar with his friends, and the wife, thinking that he'll grow out of the phase, never says a word.

No matter what defenses are used—denial, avoidance, compromise or soothing—the conflict will continue until it is addressed directly and resolved. Problems never disappear by ignoring them or wishing them away. Moreover, what doesn't get better, gets worse, because silent acceptance reinforces the mistreating mate's behavior.

Individuals who habitually avoid conflict do so not by mutual agreement, but because one or both of the partners is afraid of open conflict for any of the reasons mentioned in the previous pages. Conflict resolution cannot occur as long as problematic issues are avoided.

Contending

When an individual contends, he or she argues and debates over any issue. The central feature of contending is that every last detail must be disputed. Contending looks like this:

> *"I'm upset about what happened at your mother's last Friday..."*
> *"It was last Thursday."*
> *"O.K. last Thursday. Anyway, when she said that we should save more money..."*
> *"That's not exactly what she said."*

Contenders tear away at each other, detail by detail. No resolution can occur until contending stops.

Lack of Cooperation

Lack of cooperation can be a sign of ANS arousal or it can also be a clue that Old Scars are intruding. The person who finds it difficult to cooperate, may have a weak sense of self and believe that cooperating mean loss of identity. At the age of two, most children define their identities by opposing their parents. Saying "no" means I am me, not you. If something went awry during this stage of emotional development—if, for example, a child was never allowed to flex his individuation muscles—that person will remain stuck in this stage, and forever try to make up for what went wrong by refusing to cooperate as an adult.

Your spouse may not cooperate with you for another reason. If your mate's parents never cooperated with each other, he will be clueless on how to engage in behavior that was never demonstrated. If chronic uncooperativeness continues, after you have applied the healing techniques for this type of Old Scar (see chapter 5) and even after you have succeeded in cooling down the discussions (see chapter 7), then professional help is in order.

Controlling

Controlling behavior creates the illusion of conflict resolution, but as I said in the Big Chief/Little Indian Fight Trap, this tactic angers the spouse who is being suppressed, and creates more conflict in the long run. An inability to release the reins conceals a fear of being taken over. In order to help your mate feel safe enough to collaborate with you, you must ask for input at all phases of your conflict discussions. (for example, "What do you think?" "What do you suggest?").

Competition: Needing to Win at All Costs

Many distressed spouses approach conflict negotiations like adversaries, both trying to impose their separate agendas. This is what game theorists call the zero-sum game, in which one partner wins all and the other loses all. Couples that employ this tactic will use any or all of the Fight Traps in order to force their opponent to throw in the towel.

Why is winning so important to unhappy couples? In distressed marriages, more energy is placed on winning than on nourishing the relationship and each other. In this emotionally barren environment, both partners' egos erode; one apparent way to bolster a flailing ego is to win. Unfortunately, winning at all costs produces a vicious cycle: The winner's self-esteem is raised, but residual anger in the loser escalates conflict, which further lowers both partners' self-esteems. In order to get past this impasse, one of you must surrender. By ripping the rug out from under your power struggle, it will quickly end—a power struggle takes two to tango. When the power struggle dissolves, negotiations can proceed.

Only Wimps Give In

The belief that only wimps give in to their wives is a common male attitude. We know that males have been socialized to dominate, so it would seem that cultural conditioning underlies a man's difficulty in yielding to his wife. But there is more than cultural conditioning going on here. Behind a man's wimp phobia is another, deeper fear: the fear of being annihilated. When a man fears giving in, he believes that if he yields to his wife, even once, she will take him over forever and his testicles will hang like trophies on her nightstand. For a man with this fear, his unyielding position helps him live under the illusion that he is in control. If your husband has a wimp phobia, you need to get the point across to him that compromise is not synonymous with castration. He needs to be reassured that you want his needs to be met and it is not your intent to devour him.

No Team Players

Distressed couples are often unsuccessful in their negotiations, because they don't fight for the team. By contrast, happy couples approach the negotiation table as team members, not adversaries. Both individuals must know that a solution that is not acceptable to both, is no solution at all. They not only work as a team, they actually treat the relationship as a separate person to be cherished and respected. In all negotiations, both partners are working for a solution that is good for the relationship. If the relationship thrives, then the spouses know that they both will be happy. In unhappy relationships, however, each partner continues to live as a single person. In these cases, the individual's needs, habits, and outside friends are priority one, and the relationship receives the leftovers.

Lack of Creativity

When couples have been fighting for a while, their fights become highly patterned. I explained the scientific explanation for this in chapter 1: chronic conflict leads to a permanent state of ANS arousal, which, in turn, leads to loss of higher order cognitive functions, including creative thinking. So, we have another vicious cycle going here. So long as your fights remain unresolved, ANS arousal will prevail, which means that you cannot count on your husband to come up with a creative solution to your problem. So what can you do? First, you need to calm down; then you should be able to think creatively. Next, write down every possible solution to your problem that you can think of. If necessary, ask for ideas from friends. Calming down and thinking creatively will put you on the path to resolution.

I have now shown you every Fight Trap and faulty conflict resolution tactic uncovered in my research. These traps and tactics all have one thing in common: they are the result of acted-out anger. When anger is acted out, it invites action in return, a retaliatory behavior. Before long, couples become trapped in a web of revenge and counter revenge.

The important thing to keep in mind is that no matter what Fight Traps or faulty resolution tactics you favor, sooner or later, they all turn up the heat of your conflicts. The more heated are the fights, the more male withdrawal occurs; and, the more male withdrawal there is, the greater the conflict.

I know it is not going to be easy to give up your Fight Traps and faulty resolution tactics. But, since you are invested in saving your relationship, you have no choice but to give them up. Here's how you can do this: First, make sure that you have identified your faulty resolution tactics and Fight Traps; next, make the resolution to eliminate them. And from now on, whenever you are angry, pause before you react. This will give you the chance to stop yourself from falling into old, bad habits.

Once you have eliminated your Fight Traps and faulty resolution tactics, you will probably feel ready to roll up your sleeves and start negotiating. Not so fast. Fasten your seat belt for a major relationship hotbed: The Sex Wars.

4

Battle of the Bulge: The Sex Wars

I have said so far that most relationship warfare occurs when women complain and nag and men withdraw. There is one arena, however, in which the tables are often turned. Sex. In the first part of the chapter, I explain why heated conflicts throw cold water on a woman's sex drive. Next I discuss how a lack of understanding of the differences between male and female sexuality lead to specific types of conflicts. And, finally, I examine Sex War Games, the heated sexual arguments that usually mask other nonsexual issues.

Anger and Insecurity: The Best Form of Birth Control

Many women would shed no tears if they never had sex with their partner's again; meanwhile, their husbands chase them, begging and pleading for sex. The battle of the bulge affects millions of marriages, and is the main area in which men, as opposed to women, do the demanding. I am not saying that women never pursue men for sex. And, we will talk later in this chapter about what causes men to lose their sexual desire for their wives. But, for now, let's discuss the most common scenario: a husband who's hot to trot and a wife with a terminal headache.

The technical term for a low sex drive is *inhibited sexual desire* and this condition affects countless women. What is it about marriage that leaves many women bereft of sexual appetite? Lack of security.

59

The need for security is deeply imbedded in a woman's biological programming and explains why women have historically chosen men who can provide financially for them and their offspring. In this era of female financial independence, many women no longer need men to financially support them financially. However, statistical data show us that the instinct to be protected still governs a woman's choice of mate. That is, financially independent women still choose men who are even wealthier than themselves. If money talks, then biology screams.

The need for security is not just satisfied by choosing a financially successful mate; a woman also needs to feel secure within her relationship or marriage. When a woman feels worried that the union won't survive (as occurs in a climate of chronic conflict), her body automatically turns off from sex. The last thing she wants is a baby without a father to support it. And while she can have sex and avoid pregnancy, thanks to birth control, her biological programming doesn't realize this. This explains why women who are in the throes of relationship distress experience a sexual shutoff long before they can think about inserting their diaphragms.

Men as Emotional Providers

In order to feel secure in her relationship, a woman needs more than a climate that isn't riddled with arguments. She also needs the guarantee that her partner will stay with her forever. This guarantee was, until recently, satisfied through the traditional institution of marriage, which precluded divorce. But, today, divorce has become so common that it creates a basic insecurity in women. As a consequence, in order to feel safe, women now require an additional assurance: that their relationship will last, "till death do us part." Since that assurance is no longer derived from the external control of society (marriage is no longer indissoluble), it has to be granted by the man. And the only way that a man can persuade his partner or wife of his total commitment is through frequent reminders of his devotion. What was taken for granted in the past, must be explicitly restated, again and again. In other words, the form and scope of providing that is expected from men has drastically expanded. I believe that this new expectation is a mutation of our built-in biological need to be protected and provided for.

Reassuring his partner of his eternal devotion and love is only the first way that a man provides emotional security. The next step consists in giving his partner evidence that his words of love are not empty sounds intended to make her sexually aroused. These melodies and their intended effects will have a short life if a man does not consistently demonstrate to his partner how important she is to him. When he listens to her feelings —positive or negative—and shows that he cares for her needs, a woman feels that he loves her and wants to stay with her forever.

Even more emotional providing is required. If a man wants to create a total sense of security in his partner, he must also learn to communicate his own negative feelings to her. When a man is silent, a woman worries that he is accumulating a mountain of resentments, and that he may, one day, up and leave her. By being apprised regularly of his emotional state, she can help him purge these feelings through her understanding, and, if needed, she can change the aspects of her behavior that cause his negative feelings. His consistent feedback provides her with a sense of control over the emotional climate of the relationship, which, in turn, provides a deep sense of security.

When a woman's intimacy needs are not being answered by her partner, when she does not feel responded to, when there is no mutual communication, when there is a climate of indifference, and of course, when there is too much conflict and resentment, her biological warning light goes on and her sex drive clicks off. Her biology tells her: This man does not feel safe any longer. I don't know whether this relationship will last. If we will be separating, the last thing I want is a child. This point can't be stressed enough: A woman's sex drive fizzles when she feels emotionally insecure or angry with her mate.

Unfortunately, the emotional connection that a woman needs in order to feel turned on just happens to require a form of relating that men—through no fault of their own—are not trained to provide. So, you begin to see why millions of married women lack sexual desire and why conflicts arise in this arena. Don't get me wrong. I am not saying that women should not wish for greater emotional connection. All I am saying is that society hasn't trained men to fulfill this new cultural expectation. But, don't worry, your partner will be an expert Emotional Provider before I'm finished with him.

If men want their partners to be sexually open to their ardent approaches, and grant willingly the sexual embrace they crave, they will follow my advice. Otherwise, they will be sexually frustrated and locked in futile fights over sex.

Sexual arguments may also arise from a misunderstanding of the nature of male sexuality, the subject I next discuss.

Security Versus Variety

One of the biggest insecurity triggers, and a potent source of marital conflict, arises when a woman does not understand male sexual biology. I remember overhearing a conversation between two men that went like this:

Mike: "Have you ever been so sick that you turned your wife down?"
Fred: "Once I was so sick I turned her down."
Mike: "I could have a 105 fever and I wouldn't turn my wife down."
Fred: "I said sick!"

This conversation expresses the essence of male sexual biology. In each ejaculation, 300 million critters are sent swimming upstream to meet only one egg. Once that egg is fertilized, a woman is out of commission for nearly a year. But for the rest of his life, a man can impregnate a new woman each and every day (and twice on Sunday). Men have endless supplies of sperm, and the sperm is often manufactured until death. Women have a limited number of eggs, can only become impregnated a few days each month, and can only reproduce for a portion of their lives.

In order to ensure the continuance of the species, male sexual biology was designed so that they can impregnate as many females as possible. A man's sexual biology is like the supermarket grocery scanner. The goal: process as much merchandise as quickly as possible. But what does all this mean in modern relationship terms? Simply, that men are not wired for monogamy. It's their love for their partners that keeps them faithful despite tremendous biological programming. The way men express their love is by seeking sexual variety within the relationship. They often want sex in different locations and in kinky ways or positions. Some even like their partners to dress up like other women. Women often react to these requests with hurt. Why aren't I enough for you? You don't truly love me. Actually, by attempting to accommodate his biological urges with his partner, rather than seeking satisfaction elsewhere, a man is saying, "I love you."

I know that all this biology talk sounds like I am reducing humans to apes—or sperm and eggs. By exaggerating a little, I am trying to help you to understand how the basic differences between men and women's sexuality fuels sexual conflict. Understanding the biological underpinnings of your sexual battles, is the first step toward resolution.

Different Sexual Tastes

Now let's move beyond biology to see if we can understand what else may be causing your sexual battles. Very often, couples conflict over differing sexual tastes: One likes oral sex, while it's not the other's cup of tea; a husband likes anal sex, but his wife starts packing whenever the subject comes up. Neither partner is right or wrong, but differing values and tastes are often a source of great conflict. When couples get locked in struggles surrounding their particular bone—or should I say boner— of contention, these fights can get very nasty.

Only one year after Carol and John tied the knot, Carole's stomach was in knots. John had been working late for months (hoping to land a management position in his accounting firm), and even on his "off" time his nose was buried in records. What's more, he had developed a strange sexual disorder, which Carole called "premature intercourse." He rushed into sex before she was ready, finished the "job" quickly, then sank into a steady snore, drooling into his pillow. At first, Carole felt hurt and drenched her own pillow with tears. But soon her hurt transformed to anger.

One night, after John had his orgasm, she tapped him on the shoulder, and snarled through her curled upper lip, "Say, Mr. Accountant...ever heard about the substantial penalties for early withdrawal?"

"Very funny. Since you're such an expert...you must know why they call getting married 'tying the knot.'"

"Edify me!"

"That's what happens to a man's dick!"

Carole and John's sexual conflicts have become what I call Sex War Games. But don't be fooled; when sex has become your battleground, it's no game.

Sex War Games

Have you ever wondered why many couples resort to playing out their resentments in the sexual arena? Research shows that of all human relationships, marriage produces the most intense emotional reactions, especially anger. When anger enters the scene, you've got problems because, if you are like most people, you don't know how to express your anger constructively. As I said before, most people *act* on their anger, which invites action in return—usually revenge or retaliation. Revenge and retaliation are behavioral paybacks ("I'll get even with you because you did this to me.") The goal is to hit each other below the belt. And, you guessed it, slamming each other sexually is the ultimate below the belt blow.

Female Sex War Games

Elaine is hot—not sexually—but under the collar. For five years she has been trying to get Patrick to understand that she needs more preparation before intercourse. By this point, she is so fed up and tired of arguing with this man who doesn't get it that she has decided to get even—she will refuse him sex and teach

him a little lesson along the way. On Sunday morn-
ing, John offered to do the dishes, a sure sign that his
arousal had reached atomic proportions. Now was her
chance.

As he dried the last dish, Patrick smiled and said,
"Honey, how about a little nookie?"

"How about a little appetizer before the entree!"
she snarled, as she sorted the laundered socks.

"What's that supposed to mean?" he said, growing
beet red.

"I mean, no sex until I get some decent foreplay."

"I give you foreplay.

"Give me a break. You're one of the original minute
men!"

"Why can't you admit that you're freakin' frigid. My
other girlfriends never complained," he shouted.

"They were too busy faking it to complain!"

Placing Patrick on a bread and water sexual diet is
Elaine's way of punishing him. For centuries, the only power
a woman had was her sexuality. In the play *Lysistrata* by
Aristophanes, the Athenian women refused sex to end a war.
Throughout the ages, women have been able to force men to
slay dragons, rob banks, marry them—or whatever else they
wanted. Despite the fact that modern women have more power
than in previous eras, many women still handle their sexuality
like a power tool. You can't believe how many times a week
I hear unhappily married wives tell me, "I'll fix him, I won't
give him any." Another variant of the "I won't give him any"
approach is the "I won't give him oral sex" or "I won't fix
myself up for him." Wives who use this form of revenge don't
realize that they are actually punishing themselves, because
revenge begets revenge.

Male Sex War Games

Men rarely withhold sex as a way of obtaining revenge against their wives. (Even if they wanted to say no to sex, they have to contend with 300 million sperm urging them to take the plunge!) So, how do most men get even with their partners?

We know that women become hurt and angry when their intimacy needs are not met. Men become angry and prone to revenge when their needs for recognition and appreciation aren't being met. You can see the scenario. The woman, feeling that her partner isn't meeting her emotional or sexual needs, starts to complain about his behavior. There goes the man's needed recognition and admiration. I am not speaking now about whether or not he deserves recognition. All I am saying is that when men feel bitched at by their wives, two things happen: (1) They lose motivation to give their partners what they want (foreplay, more cuddling, better communication); and (2) They seek appreciation outside the relationship, usually in the form of an affair. If you ask a man why he had an affair, 99 percent of the time it was not because he wasn't getting enough sex; it was because he wasn't receiving enough appreciation from his partner.

Sex as the Battleground For Nonsexual Issues: How to Read Between the Sheets

When one or both partners are engaged in Sex Wars, I always suspect that something else is on the fritz in the marriage. No matter what the overt sexual struggle is, Sex War Games are often symbolic expressions of other underlying issues, such as a fear of intimacy, dependency, abandonment, and/or loss of control.

67

Jack loved his wife, but there was only one problem. He wanted nearly constant sex and his wife wasn't willing to accommodate him. Soon, he stopped asking her for sex and began having multiple affairs. Evonne was in a state of despair. She thought Jack wasn't attracted to her anymore, and she couldn't understand why he stopped approaching her for sex. She tried to do the approaching, attempted to introduce sexual variety, and had a total makeover. All to no avail. The couple came to me on the verge of divorce.

It was clear that Jack's need for constant and varied sex had a deeper meaning. It was time for some bedroom detective work, so I used my Reading Between the Sheets technique to figure out what Jack's sexual insatiability really meant. I asked him:

How did he feel when he didn't have as much sex as he liked?

How did he feel when he fulfilled his desires with strange women? Did this satisfy him?

What was he missing in the marriage, if anything?

What was he missing within himself?

What hole was he trying to fill (no pun intended) by having sex with numerous women?

By delving into Jack's background, I discovered that his father was a womanizer and that he had abandoned Jack and the family when Jack was very young. By following in his father's philandering footsteps, Jack unconsciously lived with his father at his side. So his acts of infidelity were driven by the unconscious wish to fill his inner void. The problem was that by cheating on his wife, he was jeopardizing the love that was waiting for him at home. When Jack understood this point, a miracle occurred. He was able to give up his extracurricular affairs and lived, literally, happily ever after, from that day forward.

The point to keep in mind here is that sexual conflicts are rarely about what they seem. Take as another example, the issue I promised to discuss earlier in this chapter—the battle of the bulge in reverse. Steve was a man who had lost all his sexual desire for his wife. On the surface, it was easy to assume theirs was a sexual problem. Maybe his wife Joanne had let herself go, maybe sex had become routine, maybe he had too much stress at work. I resisted the temptation to assume that this was the case. Once again, I used my Reading Between the Sheets technique and asked such questions as:

How long has the problem been going on?

What has changed in the couple's life and relationship?

Was sex ever good between them? If so, when did it deteriorate?

I learned that their sex life had been fine until the birth of their first child. But Steve's deflated drive wasn't caused by the usual culprits (unresolved anger, stress, illness, exhaustion, or the fact this his wife had become less attractive). So we needed to explore further how the birth of his child was related to his "limp loins" syndrome. Steve recalled a childhood memory in which his mother was standing in front of him in a daffodil-colored dress. He remembered feeling a rush of sexual sensations and then felt struck by a bolt of guilt. Now, we had the key to the puzzle. When Joanne became "mother," his unconscious guilt over being attracted to his own mother caused him turn off sexually to his wife. When Steve was able to recognize the deeper issue that was operating, when he realized that it was no sin to have felt attracted to his own mother, he was then able to allow himself to, once again, feel attraction for his wife.

Reading Between the Sheets is like peeling the layers of an onion. On the first layer, we discover that sexual battles often reflect deeper marital issues that have nothing to do with sex. Then, when we peel off the next layer, we discover that heated sexual conflicts are fueled by other, deeper scars from childhood. In the next chapter, I will systematically address these Old Scars.

5

Battle Scars: How Childhood Wounds Cause Chronic Conflict and How to Heal Them

Chronic marital fighting is caused by the Old Scars of childhood. In this chapter, I will help you identify the specific early wounds that are creating your relationship distress and show you effective ways to heal them.

I speak of effective healing, because, left to its own devises, the unconscious mind has an ineffective way of attempting to heal our psychological traumas: to replay, with our partner, the painful events of the past in the hope of achieving a better outcome this time around. Unfortunately, our efforts usually fail, and bitter arguments are the sad result. But our need to heal drives us to try again and again, to no avail. This leads to fight repetition, when the same fights occur regularly, and intense arguing—the two clues that Old Scars lurk beneath the surface and are adding fuel to your fights.

Repetition: The First Clue

The first way we re-create our early traumas is by choosing a mate who resembles the parent who was the source of our pain. Realize that even the most beloved parent will unintentionally fail and even traumatize his or her child. I know you may be thinking, "I didn't choose my husband, because he's like my father or mother. I picked him because he has great buns, or makes a nice macaroni salad...." These are the conscious aspects of mate selection. But, in actuality, mate selection is primarily driven by the unconscious motivation to choose someone who possesses traits that resemble the parent who injured us. I call this Setting the Stage. We set the stage not because we are gluttons for punishment, but because the unconscious has a master plan: to replay our childhood traumas with a person who symbolizes the parent who injured us; and to work for a "happy ending" to that trauma.

Janel's father abused her verbally. Not surprisingly, she married a man who belittled her daily. She came to see me, depressed, not understanding why she was treated so horribly by her husband.

By marrying a verbally abusive man, Janel unconsciously hoped to transform him into a person who treated her with respect and love. If she can pull this off, it will feel as if she succeeded in making her father come around— and her original trauma will be healed.

The plan looks good on paper, but rarely works in real life, for two reasons. First, when we choose partners who resemble our parent(s), we soon discover that our mates are incapable of providing the emotional responses we need, precisely because they are damaged or limited in the exact same areas that our parents were.

The second reason our healing attempts fail is that we adopt, with our spouse, the same strategies that we employed with our parents. And, since our methods didn't succeed with our parents, they sure aren't going to hit the jackpot with our mates. We soon feel frustrated, hurt, and furious. But, since our unconscious goal is to heal at any cost, we stay in the ring and keep swinging. The need to engage in repeated healing attempts is so universal that it actually has a name: the Repetition Compulsion.

Intensity: The Second Clue

Fight intensity is another clue that unfinished business lurks beneath the surface of your fights. Each time you fight the same fight and lose, you are more aggravated than the time before. But, there is another reason for the intensity of your reactions. When a marital crisis occurs, the mind associates the current incident with the emotionally charged, traumatic events of your childhood. This explains why fireworks are going off inside you even though the current event doesn't seem to warrant such an explosive reaction. This intensification process is similar to a small storm that picks up force as it draws moisture from its sweep across the Great Lakes.

Bob repeatedly checks his office messages when he is out with Mary. Mary becomes increasingly agitated by this behavior and finally blows up at him.

Why is she so furious over a seemingly innocuous action? Because this experience with her date triggered memories of her mother who never had time for her; so that when a trivial incident occurred in the present, it triggered that already overloaded circuit in her brain, and she blew. Such associations usually occur without any conscious awareness. Before we go farther, let's determine whether your arguments are being fueled by Old Scars. Take the following test.

The subjects that we fight about are repetitive in nature.   *Yes or No.*

I find myself and/or my partner becoming intensely upset over little things and I can't understand why.   *Yes or No.*

I find myself and/or my partner using the same words, explanations, and fighting tactics during our spats, even though these methods never work.   *Yes or No.*

I always end up with the same feelings before, during, and after our fights.   *Yes or No.*

Our fights seem familiar to me, but I can't put my finger on why.   *Yes or No.*

I feel that there is a scripted nature to our fights and that I can actually predict their same sorry outcome.   *Yes or No.*

I remember fighting with my parent(s) and feeling the same emotions that I feel now when I fight with my mate.   *Yes or No.*

The feelings that I have after a fight with my partner, remind me of how I felt as a kid.   *Yes or No.*

If you answered yes to more than one of the questions above, Old Scars are causing your fights. But you still may feel at a loss to understand what piece of your history is being played out through your marital conflicts. It is often difficult to determine the issues that underlie your arguments because the fight content operates like a smoke screen. When you are arguing over dirty socks or pots and pans, it is very difficult to abstract from these concrete subjects and see what is "underneath" your fights.

To assist in this process, I have developed a technique that I call Drawing a Fight Map, which enables you to strip away the overt fight content. Just as a restorer strips the outer layers of paint to reveal the original finish, you can go beneath the outer layer (the overt content) of your fight to reveal the underlying traumas that lurk below.

Stripping Away the Fight Content

In order to determine what traumas lie beneath your overt fight (the who did what to whom), you need to flesh out, on paper, the emotional mapping of the conflict. To do this, you must forget the apparent content of the fight— the chilly Chinese food, the rushed foreplay— and study, instead, the emotional content.

Let me show you one of Nancy and Phil's overt fights. Then I will draw upon their example to explain how you can strip away the content of your fights.

The Overt Fight

"Why can't you take me out sometimes? Would it kill you to make me happy?" Nancy whined.

"No, it wouldn't kill me!" Phil snapped.

"So, what's your problem?"

"God, I'm so busy with work and you're worried about stupid outings!"

"It's not stupid. It's important to me and that should matter to you!"

"You matter, why do you think I work as hard as I do!"

"What's work got to do with my feelings? You don't care about me at all."

"That's right. I don't care about you at all. I don't stay out drinking. I don't cheat, but I don't care!" John shouted as he stormed from the room.

"God, I can't talk to you. You just won't listen!

Drawing a Fight Map

Step One: Chart the Emotional Course of the Fight

In the first step, think of one of your common fights. For the moment, forget the content of the fight and focus on the feelings the fight stirs in you. Write down these feelings.

Let's see how Nancy and Phil stripped away the overt fight content to reveal the emotional mapping of their issue.

From Nancy's perspective: I want something from Phil. He makes excuses as to why he can't give me what I want. I get angry. He becomes more defensive. I get angrier. He digs in his heels even further. I feel hurt that he doesn't love me enough to listen and change the behaviors that annoy me. So I press harder and harder, and he withdraws further and further into excuses and denial.

From Phil's perspective: when Nancy wants something from me, she orders me and manipulates me. She gives me no freedom whatsoever. I have to do exactly as she wants or else she's furious. I feel angry, like a trapped animal. I feel like running to escape her rage and demands.

Step Two: Does the Fight Stir Feelings That You Experienced in Childhood?

Next, ask yourself, "Does the fight with my mate create the same feelings I felt as a child?" Write these feelings down. Then, ask yourself, "Who triggered these feelings in me?"

Let's see what Nancy and Phil came up with for this step.

Nancy: She recalled feeling impotent, frustrated, hurt, and angry when she tried—unsuccessfully—to get her father to respond to her.

Phil: He felt controlled by his mother and enraged at

how she forced him to do her will. Whenever he defied her, he had to suffer her fury and threats of abandonment.

Step Three: Recall a Specific Childhood Memory

Next, uncover an early memory in which you felt the way you feel when you argue with your mate. With whom were you struggling? What happened? How did the fight play out? Write this down.

Here's how Nancy and Phil handled this step.

Nancy: She recalled pleading with her father to come to at least one of her baseball games. He never showed. She begged and cried, but he never relented.

Phil: He remembered his mother forcing him to clean his room on a sunny day. When he resisted, she shouted at him and locked him in his room without supper.

Step Four: What Type of Treatment Did You Yearn For From Your Parent(s) (Your Happy Ending)?

Finally, and most importantly, ask yourself, "How did I wish my struggles with my parent(s) had worked out? Did I wish that my parent(s) would apologize, see my point of view? Did I wish my parent(s) would compromise?" Clearly identify your desired outcome. Write this down.

Let's return to Nancy and Phil for this last step.

Nancy: She wished that her father would have responded to her requests, at least sometimes.

Phil: He needed to feel free to assert himself without being punished.

♡ ♡ ♡

Once you have identified the treatment you desired from your parent(s), you have a fairly clear understanding of what your mind is hoping to accomplish in your fights with your mate (your happy ending).

The question now becomes, why don't most of us succeed in obtaining our happy endings? Why, for example, hasn't Nancy succeeded in obtaining what she needs from Phil?

Remember, Phil is just like Nancy's father. And she relates to him the way she related to her dad. For example, she used to scream, yell, pout, or whine at her father, without result. Since Phil resembles her father, it doesn't take a brain surgeon to figure out why Nancy's methods aren't cutting it. The fact that she has chosen a mate like her father cannot be changed, but what can be changed is her way of dealing with him. In other words, this aspect of the repetition compulsion (adopting the same strategies that she used with her father) is under Nancy's control. And, if she wishes to achieve her happy ending, she will modify her way of relating to Phil. The two principles that follow will help Nancy—and you—chart a new course of action.

To Achieve Your Happy Ending

One: Know Your Mate's Old Scars

If you are in the dark when it comes to what makes your mate tick, you risk to unwittingly rip open his Old Scars, in which case he will be nursing his own wounds and will be unavailable to resolve your conflicts. If necessary, redo the last exercise, and answer the questions as you believe your mate would. This process will help you identify his early wounds.

When Nancy did this, she recalled that Phil's mother's rearing methods fell into the "My way or the highway" approach. Hence, his early wound relates to never having been given sufficient autonomy. Without realizing it, Nancy's manner of handling her husband—demanding, pressuring, etc.—is painfully reminiscent of the way Phil's mother dealt with him. So Nancy had to face the fact that her pressure tactics were making Phil dig his heels in deeper.

The question now becomes, how can Nancy help Phil be more responsive to her? By providing him with a communication that is healing for him, by giving him the feeling of freedom. One possibility would be for Nancy to ask him for suggestions on how to solve their problem. Doing so would put him in the driver's seat, and if he feels in charge, rather than controlled, he will become more responsive to her. Understanding John's early wounds, is Nancy's first step on the road to resolving their fights, and healing her own Old Scars as well.

Two: Discuss Your Old Scars

To attenuate the intensity of your fights, you need to explain to your mate that an Old Scar is adding fuel to your fire. Directing the focus off his ego and onto historical sources minimizes the risk of ANS arousal and frees your mate to support you and resolve your conflicts, instead of defending himself.

A major turning point for Dottie and Russell occurred when I encouraged her to explain how his behavior was reminiscent of her mother. Russell was stiff and speechless, and Dottie was beet red.

"Explain to Russell what he is doing that reminds you of your mother," I urged.

"If I tried to tell my mother how I felt, she'd lock me in my room," Dottie said, tearfully.

"I didn't know that," Russell answered.

"Tell Russell specifically what he is doing that reminds you of your mother," I urged.

"When you tell me, 'Don't be upset, it's no big deal,' my blood boils....It's like my mother telling me to shut up!"

"I had no idea!" Russell paled with emotion. *"I always wanted to make life better for you than it was with your mother."*

When Russell's ego was taken off the hook—when he realized that the intensity of Dottie's pain and anger was the result of childhood traumas—he felt more willing to support her, rather than withdraw. This seemingly simple communication—telling your mate what old hurts have been activated by his behavior—has helped to curtail withdrawal reactions for most of the men in my studies. Try it yourself and see the miracles that occur.

In the following pages, I will outline the most common Old Scars and offer specific healing suggestions. Keep in mind that if Old Scars are being expressed through drug or alcohol abuse, or if physical violence has entered the scene, professional help must be sought.

<u>OLD SCAR #1</u>

"Where are you, mommy (daddy)?"
"Please pay attention to me, mommy (daddy)."

When you were young, your parents separated or divorced and you were emotionally or physically abandoned by one or both parents. Mom/Dad never had time for you, or vanished without a trace, or popped in and out at whim, or promised to visit and never showed up.

How This Old Scar Often Surfaces
in Relationship Conflicts: A, B, C, D

A) usually female: excessive clinginess
If abandonment is a part of your history, you may be clingy or possessive, demanding more of your partner's time than he is willing to give or requesting constant reassurances that you are important to him.

B) male or female: jealousy
You may feel that your mate loves another person more than you, even though you have no reason to suspect infidelity. You may feel jealous of his involvement with other people, or of the time he devotes to the kids, friends, or hobbies.

C) male or female: acting out behaviors
You or your mate may engage in behaviors designed to fill the emptiness inside: excessive drinking or spending; overeating; promiscuous sex; or extramarital affairs. If either partner's behavior is out of control, professional help is needed.

D) often male (but can occur with females): fears of intimacy or dependency
The person who was abandoned as a child may behave in ways that keep his mate at arm's distance—working compulsively, avoiding family outings or vacations, or missing family meals. The unconscious goal is to avoid intimacy at all costs in order to protect oneself: "If I am cut off emotionally, then I won't suffer when I am abandoned again."

Type of Healing Needed
For A, B

You need to know that your mate will not abandon you the way your parent(s) did. Additionally, you must feel that you are number one in your partner's eyes. Remember, it's hard for your mate to offer this message if he feels blamed for infidelity or neglect. Also, keep in mind that actions or omissions that may slightly annoy someone else will devastate you because of your history. You must tell your spouse that your accusations of infidelity or neglect have been fueled by childhood abandonments. When the blame is directed away from his ego, he won't feel impelled to defend himself and can devote his energy to offering the assurances you need. These principles also apply if the husband is the jealous partner.

Type of Healing Needed
For C

If either of you is acting out in order to fill an internal void, strong limits must be set around the unacceptable behavior. At the same time, a great deal of emotional nourishment must be provided.

Chet regularly comes home drunk and forces sex on his wife, Eva. For years, she tolerated his behavior. Then, when he fell asleep, she would search for the abandoned car, which he had been too drunk to drive home. The next day she yelled at him, but also called in sick for him, using some bogus excuse. Without knowing it, she was rewarding Chet's destructive behavior. After talking with me, we devised a plan. No sex for him if he was drunk, and no sweeping up behind him either. He would have to find the car himself and call his boss.

I instructed Eva to give him no attention whatsoever, including negative attention (yelling, screaming) when he acted badly and to stop bailing him out. The result: within a few months, he stopped drinking and cleaned up his act considerably.

The limits that Elaine imposed on her husband were firm and consistent and not presented in the form of screaming and yelling. This is an important point because even negative attention has the effect of reinforcing behavior.

In addition to ignoring inappropriate behavior, I encouraged Eva to praise Chet's positive behaviors. I know it's hard to praise someone who still continues to behave in unacceptable ways, but keep in mind that no matter how badly your partner may be behaving, there is always something that you can find to praise. You might just be so angry that you aren't noticing the good things. Even if you don't feel like it, do offer emotional support, recognition, and praise whenever your partner behaves more properly, and especially give praise for the little gains. In Eva's case, she recognized Chet for taking the responsibility to call in sick. When you praise the little gains, this encourages your partner to make bigger gains. In fact, many studies, including my own research, have shown that people change their behavior when they are rewarded, whereas punishment (nagging, yelling, screaming, etc.) has no effect on improving behavior.

Type of Healing Needed
For D

If your spouse was abandoned as a child, he still lives in fear of being abandoned again. So he backs off to protect himself, thinking that if he is emotionally detached, he won't suffer when you leave him. You need to help him see that if he isn't careful, he may arrange to make his worst fear come true: his protective mechanism may backfire because his pulling back pushes you away.

In order to heal, he needs to allow himself to connect to you. But before he can do so, he requires an emotional insurance policy that protects him against being abandoned by you. At the same time, he needs to know that whenever he feels too frightened by the closeness, you will allow him to back away, temporarily. Before withdrawing, he needs to explain that he is backing off to deal with his own fears, not to escape you or the family. You can tell him the following: "I just want to reassure you that I'm not going anywhere. I want you to also know that if you take the risk to get closer to me, I will give you breathing room any time you need it. So long as I understand why you are pulling away— to handle your own fears, not to escape me—I will happily give you your space."

<u>OLD SCAR # 2</u>

"Mommy (daddy), get off my back."

You grew up with an overly controlling or intrusive parent who told you when to do your homework, what friends you could play with, what sports you could engage in, or what hobbies you should perform.

How This Old Scar Often Surfaces
in Relationship Conflicts: A, B, C

A) male or female: tyrannical behavior
A person who felt controlled as a child will likely become a tyrant in adulthood, copying the behavior of a bossy

84

parent. Overly controlling behavior is a defense against being controlled.

B) *male or female: uncooperative behavior*

Various power struggles may crop up, and you or your partner will have difficulty yielding, compromising, or considering the other's point of view. Fights will run on forever and the tyrannical partner will use pressure and manipulation tactics in order to impose his or her desires or position.

C) *often female: excessive compliance*

If you were dominated as a child, you may behave in overtly compliant ways and allow your partner to rule you. Privately, you struggle with feelings of victimization, helplessness, or anger.

Type of Healing Needed
For A, B

The person who was dominated as a child, needs to experience the feeling of independence that was lacking in childhood. It is common for the overly controlled child to become a tyrant in adult life. (No one is going to boss me. Everything is going to be my way.) If you are on the receiving end of a tyrant, the natural reaction is to resist the commands. Before long, you become trapped in endless tugs-of-war. The challenge here is to resist digging in your heels and becoming the stubborn parent your mate grew up with. Instead, transform your mate into your consultant and regularly seek his opinion on how he recommends dealing with your conflicts. If you do this, he will feel considered and will be less likely to force his will down your throat. I know it is not a natural tendency to yield when you are fighting with someone who won't consider your position or contemplate a compromise. To declare a truce to the tug-of-war requires a lot of maturity on your part, but remember, by temporarily backing off you are providing your partner with the necessary emotional healing. Soon he will feel satisfied that his needs have been respected and will be ready to consider your needs. By backing off, you have, in fact, modeled for your partner how to respect another person's feelings. As long as you maintain the tug-of-war, you are, unwittingly, playing the role of the controlling parent, and your partner will never have a chance to heal the wound and grow up. The yielding on your part should not become a permanent solution to the conflicts. It is only temporary and is designed to provide your partner with the feeling that he can have things his way; not through winning a fight, but because you love him enough to give him the respect and consideration he never had as a kid. After a while, your partner should be more willing to give equal time to your needs.

Type of Healing Needed
For C

Your healing requires that you become an equal partner. In doing so, you may be jeopardizing your marriage, which has probably been built upon a power imbalance.

Realize that he married you because you allowed him to dominate you; and his ego thrives on feeling superior, needed, and important. How will he react to your gaining more equality? Be prepared for the risks before you assert yourself. If you decide that you are ready, go slowly. First, start talking about your need for more of a voice in the marriage—for example, participate in the financial planning or in the establishment of a budget. And be prepared for much balking on your partner's part. He may be afraid to relinquish control. His resistance may also conceal a fear that, if you become more independent, you won't need him any longer. So, as you take your full place in the marriage, you need to keep telling him how important he is to you and how much you continue to need him. If you sense that your mate is frightened by the loss of control, then make sure to keep asking for his opinions, and suggestions.

<u>OLD SCAR #3</u>

"Mommy (daddy), why can't I just play?"

You were robbed of your childhood by being forced to assume too much responsibility as a child. You might have done all the housework, or perhaps you had to care for siblings or parents who were physically ill, emotionally disturbed, or chemically dependent.

How This Old Scar Often Surfaces in Relationship Conflicts: A, B

A) usually male: irresponsible behavior
    A refusal to accept adult responsibilities: paying bills late; not keeping promises; not following the law or rules.

B) often female: overly responsible behavior
    If you assumed the caretaker role in childhood, you will probably take an overly responsible attitude in your marriage. Since your parents were unable to assume adequate responsibility for you, you would have drowned if you hadn't stayed in charge. As an adult, you continue assuming all of the duties of your household. Beneath the overly responsible attitude is a fear that life will fall apart if you give over the reins. You may also fear that your mate will not be able to handle his share of responsibility. Since you are carrying too much responsibility in the relationship, you feel resentment toward, and may fight

87

with, your partner for his not doing his share of the household tasks.

Type of Healing Needed
For A

Your partner needs to experience the fun and freedom he never enjoyed as a child. The challenge for you is not to fall into the role of the nagging and controlling parent. If you fall into this trap, your mate's need to rebel will constantly be refueled by you. The best plan is to remove yourself from the hot seat by allowing him to fall flat on his face. This is difficult to do because many of your mate's irresponsible actions will boomerang on you. You may want to take some measures to protect yourself—like setting up separate checking accounts. Once you have put your damage control in place, make sure not to bail your "kid" out when he gets into a tight spot. Let him get himself out. And make sure that you don't fall in the trap of scolding him for his mistakes—ignore them, otherwise you will be reinforcing his behavior through negative attention. If you can tolerate this process, his irresponsible actions will usually be short-lived. When he has to suffer the consequences of his acts, he will soon find that having so much fun is too big a pain.

Realize that "letting go" and not bailing your mate out will probably be especially difficult for you because your over responsibility probably re-creates patterns you learned in childhood (familiar pain).

Type of Healing Needed
For B

You need to give over responsibility to your mate gradually, until there is a more equal division of tasks. In the beginning, you will probably still need to tell your partner how you prefer the work done. You must realize, however, that men don't like being told how to perform tasks. So make sure that your suggestions do not come across as controlling or bossy. You also need to let your mate know that your "how-to" suggestions, if followed, will help you surrender the reins more easily and make you less angry at him. There is usually a fly in the ointment with this type of problem. It is not uncommon for the "do-all" type woman to become committed to someone she can't rely on and, so, giving over the reins to such a person would, in fact, be risky. If you can't count on your mate, you will need to follow the healing suggestions for Old Scar #4.

OLD SCAR #4

"Mommy and/or daddy don't care what I do."

Your partner was not given enough limits or responsibility (his parents never set a curfew, never made him do his homework or chores).

How This Old Scar Often Surfaces
in Relationship Conflicts

Many male children are treated like kings by mothers who never stop taking care of them. Men who have been raised in this way suffer from what psychoanalysts call an oral dependency, meaning that they are fixated in the oral stage of development. And these men come to marriage expecting their wives to take over where their mothers left off—kind of like switching from the right breast to the left breast. With this type of man, you are dealing with a two-pronged problem: a developmental sticking point and a culture-bound socializa-

89

tion that may be part of your mate's personality make-up. He will usually come and go as he pleases, play hard, and assume no responsibility for household chores or money management. If you are on the receiving end of this behavior, you may fall into the role of the nagging, complaining wife.

Type of Healing Needed

To help your mate become more responsible, you will gradually need to do less for him and praise him for any responsible actions he takes on his own. Don't expect him to become Mister Responsible overnight. He was, after all, rewarded as a child for not being responsible and you rewarded him too by allowing his behavior to continue until recently. Your challenge is how to make him feel rewarded for being responsible now. Humans grow when enough love and encouragement is offered. I know it may sound silly to think of your partner as a child needing positive reinforcement, and you may be thinking, "It's not my job to be his mother," but you are already being his mother by taking on most of the responsibility and nagging him like a parent. You are a negative mother to him. How about trying to be a positive mother? Remember, he will need a lot of praise from you to give up a way of being that feels pretty damn good.

If you feel like digging in your heels and not giving him what he needs, you should examine how this resistance connects to your own past. Maybe your parents tried to teach you by punishing bad behavior rather than positively reinforcing good behavior. If this is true, you may be tempted to use the same methods with your mate. If you insist upon teaching him through negative messages, punishment, and taking away what he likes, you will have a child for life. Until you can move beyond your sticking point, he won't be able to grow. Not to mention the fact that if you punish him too much, he could get

90

fed up and leave. Didn't he marry you because he knew you would fill the responsible role in your marriage? If the answer is yes, and if you decide to change the rules midstream, you have to go about this slowly and in a positive fashion. You can help your partner become more mature and responsible by adopting the following steps.

1. No more positive attention for irresponsible behavior. This includes, bailouts, clean-ups, etc.

2. No more negative attention for irresponsible behavior. This includes screaming, yelling, etc.

3. Give no attention whatsoever to immature behavior. Pretend you're deaf, dumb, and blind. (This is very hard to do when you feel like killing your mate. Just keep saying to yourself, "This is temporary, and it will work!")

4. Reward your mate's responsible behaviors with words of praise, signs of affection, and positive attention.

5. Remember to reward the baby steps. Very often wives expect overnight results (after all he is an adult.) Remember, we all must crawl before we walk. And no matter what age your mate is, if he never learned to walk on his own, he must learn to crawl now. Make sure that each tentative step is rewarded with praise.

<u>OLD SCAR # 5</u>

"Mommy (daddy), stop yelling at me."
"Mommy (daddy), stop hitting me."

How This Old Scar Often Surfaces
in Relationship Conflicts: A, B

A) *male or female*

Formerly abused people are in danger of behaving in abusive ways.

B) *usually female*

If you were abused as a child, you risk becoming a victim in adulthood.

Type of Healing Needed
For A

If you or your partner grew up with abusive parents, you probably never learned how to handle angry feelings in nondestructive ways. See chapter 9 for a complete discussion of how to communicate negative feelings properly.

If you are on the receiving end of verbal abuse, you must not reward your mate with any form of attention, which includes continuing to dialogue. When the verbal abuse begins, quietly, but firmly say, "If you want to calmly describe what I said or did that upset you, I will listen. But if you continue to insult me, I will have to leave." If this limit doesn't work, you must walk away. If you have any fear, whatsoever, that limit setting will cause your mate to become more out of control, seek professional help at once.

If you were abused as a child, you may find yourself wanting to get even with the parent who mistreated you—and you may find yourself dumping on your partner. The risk of this happening increases when your partner unconsciously reminds you of the parent whom you resent. The solution: you need to separate the angry feelings designed for your parent(s) from

92

the feelings you have for your spouse. Ideally, your spouse should become an ally in this process, by dialoguing with you. Here's how to do this:

First: Pretend that your parent is in the room.

Next: Tell your spouse what you would say to your parent if he or she were present.

Third: Identify what your partner does that reminds you of your abusive parent(s).

And, finally, after you have realized what your partner is doing to upset you, tell your partner how his behavior reminds you of your parents. In making this link, you achieve two ends: (1) Your spouse will feel less personally blamed and more willing to listen to your pain and alter his behavior; and (2) Discussing your pain with your loved one will help heal your Old Scar.

When verbal abuse has entered the relationship, it is always a good idea to seek professional help, because verbal abuse often leads to physical violence.

Type of Healing Needed
For B

Former victims are afraid to stand up for themselves, for fear of retaliation. The healing technique for A above shows how to set limits on a verbal abuser. If you have felt like a victim for a long time, professional help may be needed to help you break this cycle.

<u>OLD SCAR #6</u>

"Mommy and daddy, please stop yelling at each other."

You or your mate grew up with parent(s) who criticized, belittled, or put each other down.

**How This Old Scar Often Surfaces
in Relationship Conflicts**

male or female: argumentative behavior
 There will be very heated, unending arguments in which verbal abuse is present.

Type of Healing Needed
SEE RECOMMENDATIONS FOR OLD SCAR # 5

OLD SCAR # 7
"Daddy, don't hit mommy."
"Mommy and daddy, stop hitting each other."

**How this Old Scar Often Surfaces
in Relationship Conflicts**

male or female: behaving abusively or becoming the victim of abuse
 When a person witnesses battering during the formative years, he or she may become a batterer or a victim of battering later in life. If physical abuse exists in your relationship, seek professional help at once.

OLD SCAR # 8

"Mommy (daddy), stop touching me that way."

**How This Old Scar Often Surfaces
in Relationship Conflicts: A, B**

A) male or female: sexual shut-down

You may feel sexually numb or experience a lack of sexual interest, which are protective mechanisms.

B) male or female: sexual acting out
    If you were sexually abused as a child, you may become a sex addict, sexually unfaithful, promiscuous, or even obsessed with kinky sex.

Type of Healing Needed
For A
If you feel sexually numb Sensate Focus, described in these two paragraphs, is a good exercise to perform. The purpose of this exercise is to learn to enjoy the pleasure of being touched—without feeling pressured to become aroused. When memories and feelings associated with the earlier abuse arise, speak about this with your mate. Get out of bed (if you are there) and talk about the painful subject, as far from the bedroom as you can. You don't want to taint your bedroom with bad feelings about sex.

    When you are being touched, make a conscious point of separating, in your mind, your mate's touch from the abuser's touch. Repeat positive thoughts to yourself. For example, you might say, "My lover is touching me," "It feels good," "I want to be touched," "I am entitled to have pleasure," "My body is wonderful," etc. If this exercise, does not succeed in resolving your problem, seek professional help.

Type of Healing Needed
For B
If you or your mate are sexually acting out, these behaviors are aimed at keeping the painful feelings away. You shouldn't be forced to abruptly arrest the troublesome sexual behaviors. They will diminish naturally as you are helped to face gradually

the feelings associated with the earlier abuse and work them through. This type of work needs to be done in therapy.

OLD SCAR # 9

"You like my sister (or brother) more than me."

How This Old Scar Often Surfaces in Relationship Conflicts

male or female: feeling sided against

If you experienced sibling rivalry growing up, you may unconsciously arrange situations in which sides are taken. And, as you know, relationship conflicts result whenever you think your partner is taking another person's side or doesn't agree with your point of view.

Type of Healing Needed

If you are on the receiving end of the setup, avoid getting backed into the side-taking corner. Give the emotional message that your mate is number one and that you are always on his side. And, if you must take another person's side over your mate's, do not do it publicly. Make sure that you handle all issues where third parties are concerned when you are alone with your mate. If you must disagree, remember to preface your position with supportive statements and reminders that he is always number one. For example, your mate wants the kids to go to bed early as a punishment and you feel the punishment is too harsh. When you are alone together, this is what you might say:

"Honey, you know I think you're a great parent, but on this subject I think we need to reconsider." Start

with a positive, support statement and then position yourself as part of his team.

"You're always taking their side over mine."

"I know it hurts you when I don't agree with you."

"Yeah."

"Like when no one listened to your side and squashed you down." (Understanding goes a long way in showing you're on his side.)

"Exactly."

"I understand how bad it was for you, and that's why we have to work together as a team to make sure that the kids don't feel squashed the way you did."

It has not been my intention to lay blame on parents in this chapter. We all know that, despite their best intentions, parents make mistakes. You made mistakes, so did your parents, as did their parents. These wounds pass from generation to generation. The point is, we all come to adulthood scarred in one way or another, and, as I hope I have shown, by following my suggestions, couples can do a great deal to help each other heal Old Scars.

Let me remind you that awareness is the key to healing your Old Scars. By simply identifying what unresolved childhood issues are being re-created in your marital conflicts, and working together to resolve them, you are on the path to healing.

While marriage has the power to heal, we know also that most couples end up trapped in endless fighting cycles in which they relive, rather than heal, their childhood scars. During bitter fighting, many couples fall into endless, destructive communication potholes. In order to resolve conflicts, we must make sure that your mind is working for, not against, you.

6

How Your Head Can Be Your Own Worst Enemy: Training Your Mind to Fight for (Not against) You

Misunderstandings are the source of many fights. As you will see, how you interpret your mate's actions or words will determine whether or not a fight breaks out. In other words, your head — that is, your interpretation of what you see and hear— can be your best friend or your worst enemy. It has been repeatedly shown that unhappy couples interpret each others' communications in distorted ways. And, you guessed it, the bias swings in the most negative possible direction. In this chapter, I will explain that negatively interpreting your mate is an ANS arousal trigger and the kiss of death to conflict resolution.

Why would a perfectly normal person read a partner in the most negative light? For one thing, Old Scars taint how you interpret the world. If you were spoken to in put-downs, you will expect to hear put-downs. If you were praised, you will expect praise. In other words, we hear what we expect to hear.

The Echo Process

Since we have chosen mates who resemble our parents, we unconsciously assume that they will relate to us the way our parents did. This leads us to distort the meaning of our mates' communications so that they fulfill our expectations. I call this the Echo Process.

In a very short time, the Echo Process takes a diabolical turn: our unconscious minds actually induce our partners to treat us in ways that are familiar to us. Let's use Lucy as an example. Lucy's father was critical of her and so we know that she will be prone to hearing criticism in whatever her husband, Dan, says, whether or not the criticism was intended. Believing that criticism is coming at her all the time, she naturally responds to him in angry ways. Obviously, Dan feels angry to be falsely accused, and he begins to expect that every word out of Lucy's mouth will be an attack on him. Soon, he incorrectly reads her most innocent statements as attacks, and everything he says comes out sounding angry and attacking, just like her father!

So you see, Lucy's mind has enticed Mark to treat her the way her father did. This is just what her mind wanted. But here is where most couples get stuck: History has repeated itself (Setting the Stage); your partner treats you like your parent(s), but what happened to the happy ending? Instead of achieving a resolution to your early traumas, you feel nothing but resentment for each other.

What happens next in this atmosphere of chronic resentment? Since you are not getting love and support from your mate, you begin to engage in score keeping (I'm right and you're wrong. I won and you lost.) Winning is an uplifting experience, and without knowing it, you are shoring up your ego, which isn't getting much support from your mate.

Unfortunately, this ego-boosting maneuver is relationship busting, because it sets up a deadly vicious cycle: it fosters more ANS arousal in men, which leads to more withdrawal more anger on the wife's part, more bad chemistry and more withdrawal, more anger on the woman's part, more bad chemistry, and more withdrawal.

Read the following conversation between Nancy and

Phil, the couple we met in chapter 5, and see if you can detect how the Echo Process has set off ANS arousal in Phil.

Phil: Is tonight chicken night, already?
Nancy: Listen, if you don't like my cooking, make your own meals.
Phil: I didn't say I didn't like it. I just couldn't believe that chicken night had rolled around...you know, how fast time flies. Why are you always overreacting? You're so hysterical.
Nancy: Oh, here we go again, you're Mister Perfect. You never do or say anything wrong.
Phil (rolling his eyes): Oh God, my wife the hysteric. (He leaves the room.)
Nancy (shouting): I'd tell you to go to hell, but you're such a saint. Tell you what, (dumping the food down the disposal), why don't you ask God to make your last supper.

What happened here? Nancy, hearing criticism in her partner's opening question, ("Is tonight chicken night already?"), immediately attacked Phil. In turn, ANS arousal kicked in, and he became defensive, counterattacked, and then the fight (and the meal) went down the drain. This is where the relationship is going to end up if this couple doesn't learn to interpret each other's opening remarks properly, and stop fights before they start.

How can you train your brain not to steer you wrong? First, decide that for a trial period you will not immediately react when you feel criticized. This takes enormous will power. But, the payoff is saving your relationship. It's entirely up to you, and I promise you, the following technique has worked for the majority of couples that I have treated. If you have decided to give this a try, read on.

How to Train Your Brain to Interpret
Your Mate's Opening Statements Properly

Step One: Hold Your Horses

The next time you feel that your partner's opening remark is a criticism or an attack, don't do or say anything. You may need a break, so tell your partner that you need a minute to work something out in your head. Leave the room, if necessary.

Step Two: Take a Step Back in Time

Now, think back to your childhood, and ask yourself if your partner's remark reminds you of something from your past. Bring up any memory that seems pertinent. Who said what to you? What was that person's body language, tone of voice, and facial expression when he or she said what upset you.

Step Three: Take a Hard Look at Reality

Ask yourself, were my mate's words, actions, body language, tone of voice, or facial expressions similar to the behavior of the person in my childhood memory? Is there any chance (even 1 percent) that there could be another explanation for his actions or words? Is it possible that I have misinterpreted him? If you have the slightest question that there could be another, more positive interpretation, give your partner the benefit of the doubt.

Step Four: Check Out Your Suspicion

Now you can return to your partner and use a technique that I call the Checkout. No, I don't mean that you or your partner should check out of the relationship. I mean that since we decided there is the possibility that you may have been hearing your partner in an overly negative light, you need to Check Out your suspicion that you might be wrong.

Step Five: Smooth Any Ruffled Feathers (Use As Needed)
This incident (your upset, your leaving the room) may have sparked ANS arousal in your partner so make sure to smooth his ruffled feathers. To do this, you can tell him what the current incident reminded you of and explain that the intensity of your reaction stemmed from other issues. This technique is very effective in heading off ANS arousal and male withdrawal, because the focus of the blame is taken off of him and is redirected onto more neutral territory, such as your history.

How did Nancy and Phil put the five steps into practice? I'll show you how.

Replay of the Chicken Delight Nightmare: I

Phil: Is tonight chicken night, already?
Nancy: Honey, I'm having a reaction to that question. Give me a moment. (Hold Your Horses
Nancy realizes that Phil's remark reminded her of her father, who always put her down. (Take a Step Back in Time)
Next, she reviews the vocal tone and body language that accompanied his statement and realized that they were neutral. (Take a Hard Look at Reality).

Now, she is ready to resume the conversation with him.

Nancy: I just want to be sure. Are you saying that you don't like my chicken? (Check Out Your Suspicion)
Phil (raising his voice): Of course not. Why do you

always think I'm criticizing you?
Nancy: Honey, I understand you feel upset. Do you want to know why I misread you? (Smooth Any Ruffled Feathers)
Phil: O.K.
Nancy: You know how my dad always told me I couldn't do anything right.... Well, I'm so used to being put down by him that I misinterpreted what you said. (Smooth Any Ruffled Feathers)
Phil: I get it now.
They hug and the misunderstanding is resolved.

With practice, you will be able to perform steps one through three in the blink of an eye, and without leaving the room or interrupting the flow of conversation. When you reach this level of proficiency, you will probably be able to move directly into the Checkout and skip the other steps. The following is an example of what I mean.

Replay of the Chicken Delight Nightmare: II

Phil: Is tonight chicken night, already?
Nancy: I just want to be sure. Are you saying that you don't like my chicken? (Check Out Your Suspicion)
Phil: No, not at all, it's that I am surprised how time flies.
Nancy: You would tell me if you didn't like my chicken? (Check Out Your Suspicion again)
Phil: Yes, I would, and I do like your chicken.
Nancy: Which part of my meat do you prefer? (She giggles.)
Phil: Well, you know I'm a breast man, but I also like the thighs, and especially the neck. (He walks

closer.)
Nancy: Are you hungry now?
Phil: I could do with a bite. (He takes her in his arms
and nibbles her neck affectionately.)

As you can see, by employing the Checkout technique, the opening remark was properly interpreted and a fight was avoided. Remember, fights are like railroad tracks: If you switch onto the wrong track, there will be a crash of head cars; but, if you switch to the proper track (by correctly interpreting an opening remark) a crash can often be avoided.

Excessive Personalization

In addition to negative distortions, chronically conflicted partners must weed out another type of cognitive distortion: excessive personalization.

Doreen's husband has been coming home late from work for the past few weeks. She automatically assumed that Leroy's behavior was directed at her (personalizing). Once Doreen began personalizing, her mind was off and running, concocting interpretations that tortured her half to death. (He's found another woman. He doesn't find me attractive any more.) When such ideas emerged, she felt hurt and angry. Next Doreen acted out her anger (whining, complaining, criticizing, attacking), which triggered ANS arousal and withdrawal in her partner; his withdrawal, in turn, added fuel to her belief that he didn't love her anymore, and, in no time, a major war was in progress.

While men find it hard to accept responsibility when

they cause emotional pain, women are all too quick to personalize and hold themselves accountable when there is no reason to do so. For goodness' sake, and for the sake of your relationship, always assume that you are unnecessarily personalizing, and before becoming reactive, Checkout Your Suspicion to make sure that your perceptions are correct.

There are, of course, occasions in which a Checkout will confirm the accuracy of your interpretation. In such cases, you will need to use the conflict resolution techniques discussed in chapters 8 through 10.

Once you have learned how to train your brain to fight for you, not against you, you are almost ready to sign a permanent peace treaty with your partner. But first, before any negotiations techniques can be acquired, you must learn the elements of relationship Climate Control.

7

The Battle Ax: How Women Can Use Climate Control Techniques to End Relationship Fighting

Bernadette awoke in a sunny mood. Today was her day to lunch in her favorite cafe with her best friend, Sally. Her mood rapidly clouded when she tripped on her husband's dirty jeans, crumpled on the floor beside the bed. As she walked to the bathroom, she stumbled on a minefield of more dirty laundry. Inside the bathroom, she found a hairball in the sink and wet towels thrown inside the tub. Her anger began rising like mercury in the sun. She took a deep breath, counted to fifty, and headed for the kitchen, where she found the table littered with crumbs and coffee spills, the milk carton saluting her from the counter, and a pile of dirty dishes. Suddenly, her anger thermometer shot over the top. She yanked the phone from its cradle and pounded out Peter's office number.

He answered with a cheerful, "Hello."

"You've done it again!" she shouted.

"What's your problem?"

"I'm not your freakin' maid, that's my problem. How many times have I asked you to clean up after yourself?"

"You're off the wall, you know that. Maybe you should see a shrink."

"You've got balls calling me a nut, you pig!" she

shouted into a dead line.

Now Bernadette was in a very, very bad mood.

"Life's a bitch and then you marry one" is a saying that's plastered on truck bumpers across America. Where bumper stickers don't exist, you will probably find men huddled around campfires uttering complaints about the Battle-Ax who is back in her teepee stewing (and I don't mean tomatoes). I suspect that if people lived on the moon, we would find this slogan embroidered in the sky.

Many married women are angry over having to carry the bulk of domestic tasks, in addition to their outside jobs. And the icing on top of the cake (that they baked from scratch) is the fact that their emotional needs aren't being met. And when a woman is upset, she makes sure her partner knows about it. Unfortunately, the expressive nature of the female gender role is the spark that ignites the physiologically hyper-reactive male. I'm not saying that you need to button it when it comes to issues that are troubling you. What I am saying is that before you can even think about tackling your relationship beefs, you must send ANS arousal and withdrawal behaviors packing. Otherwise you'll be attempting to negotiate with the back of your partner's head! Bottom line: before attempting to negotiate, you must first cool down the relationship climate with the following relationship Climate Control techniques.

The Elements of Relationship Climate Control

There are seven basic Cool-Down principles.

The Team Comes Ahead of the Individual Players

Happy couples fight for the team, not for the individual players. They strive for a win/win situation, rather than a win/lose outcome. If either partner sees that a conflict is not going well for the team, one or the other will yield, compromise, postpone discussions, or do whatever is needed for the team to win. This means that these couples systematically avoid the Fight Traps that we discussed in chapter 3, all of which escalate conflict.

Knowing When to Shut Up

Happy couples know how to leave the "better left unsaid," unsaid. In unhappy relationships, partners practice the "honesty is the best policy" approach. I don't know who was responsible for inventing that phrase, because, without a doubt, it is the biggest fallacy ever to be foisted upon marriage. Don't misunderstand me. I'm not saying that you should lie. What I am saying is that, sometimes, saying everything can do more harm than good. I always tell my couples: "Before speaking, ask yourself, 'If I say what I wish to say, will it be helpful to my mate and our relationship?' If your answer is 'No,' then button it."

When to Let It Go and When to Take It to the Mat

In unhappy relationships, every issue is considered a federal case. Tony Robbins calls this "majoring in minor things." Oftentimes distressed couples do this because unresolved issues and residual resentment (as well as disturbed body chemistry) are adding fuel to the fire. Before they know it, they're literally screaming over nothing.

Sometimes, making a federal case over small issues occurs because couples are, more or less consciously, trying to avoid discussing the real issues that are bothering them. Since they lack appropriate conflict resolution skills, they know a fight will break out if they try to address the true problems. This avoidance leaves everyone edgy and prone to snapping over little things.

*Sarah likes to think of herself as a forgiving per-
son who doesn't let little things get to her. Every time
Steve leaves his shoes in the middle of the floor, she is
annoyed but doesn't think such a petty thing is worth
mentioning. When he criticizes her cooking in front of
his mother, she tells herself, through clenched teeth,
not to make a big deal over nothing. Then one night,
Steve arrived home five minutes late for dinner, and
Sarah, the queen of forgiveness, began screaming like
a madwoman, and flinging every piece of dinnerware
across the room—winning the china Frisbee champ-
of-the-year award.*

Avoiding conflict discussions can blow up in your face.
When anger is not discharged in the moment, an emotional
residue, similar to soap scum, lingers; and that accumulated
residue can foment (not foament) an explosion when you least
expect it. So when an issue is important, it must be addressed,
not buried.

How do you know when an issue is important enough
not to drop? I always tell my clients, "If it bothers you, it's
important." If you tend to sweep all issues under your emotional
rug, then assume, at least in the beginning, that everything is
important. You will soon know what is and is not worth getting
riled about. Rule of thumb: deal with the issue promptly or
let it go. But, make sure that if and when you decide to let an
issue go that you are not simply avoiding it and burying it in a
shallow grave.

When to Call a Permanent Truce on Certain Topics
Happy couples avoid discussions of hot topics that have no

bearing on the relationship (for example, political differences). Unhappy couples, by contrast, have a knack of returning to their areas of difference, forever trying to impose their opinions on each other. When this is done, all that gets imposed on each other are bad feelings.

Give the Benefit of the Doubt

I have spoken often about how your mind can be your own worst enemy by assigning a negative slant to your mate's communications. The technical term for this is called *mind reading with negative affect*, and unhappy couples have Ph.D.'s on this one. Happy couples, by contrast, give the benefit of the doubt to their mates, assuming the best, not the worst, possible interpretation of their mates' words, actions, and gestures. This positive bias sets an upbeat tone to the relationship so that a self-fulfilling prophecy occurs. When you expect to hear positives, these are the types of communications you invite. Keep practicing the Checkout exercises in chapter 6, which will teach you how to give your mate the benefit of the doubt—a vital relationship-climate cooler.

Red-Alert: Recognize Relationship Danger Zones

Happy couples are experts at recognizing their Relationship Danger Zones (physical or emotional exhaustion, illness, loss or death of a relative or friend, or having been angered in the recent past) and making sure to avoid important discussions until one or both of the partners is less vulnerable.

Daily Bread: Maintain the Five to One Ratio

In happy relationships, couples maintain a five-to-one ratio of positive to negative communications. The marital researchers Gottman and Silver have found that for every one negative word, interaction, or communication delivered in a day, there are five loving messages offered to counterbalance the negative. If this ratio of five parts positive to one part negative is not maintained, a relationship quickly dissolves.

Distressed partners often tell me that their mates don't perform five praiseworthy acts in a year, let alone in a day. If you feel this way, I can assure you that your anger is blinding you from seeing the good before your eyes. Nursing your anger, and refusing to see your mate's positive behaviors is a twisted form of self-protection If you see the good, you might have to let down your guard and risk being hurt again. As long as you feel angry, you have your armor to protect you. But, is all this anger really a protection? In the short-run it may feel like it; ultimately, using anger as armor is destructive in that it sustains the war and prevents you from getting the love you need.

How about trying something with me? Don't let down your guard. Don't trust your mate. Even hold on to your feelings of anger, if you wish, but, temporarily, put them in your psychological bottom drawer. You can always pull the anger out of the drawer at any moment. Now, for the sake of your relationship, ask yourself, "If I weren't so angry, what could I praise in my partner's actions?" Write these things down.

Next, verbalize the praise to your mate. When you deliver the praise, remember that you don't have to let down your guard or trust your mate. Just deliver the praise and watch what happens.

General Cool-Down Techniques for When Conflict Strikes

In addition to cool-down basics, you need to know how to cool the climate when either of you is hot under the collar.

111

Keep a Calm Tone

Gottman and Silver also found that unhappy couples can be distinguished from unhappy couples by the tone of voice they use when speaking with each other. Chronically conflict couples speak to each other in harsh, whining, sarcastic, and irritable tones, whereas happy couples never speak to each other in these ways. Did unhappy couples develop these harsh tones after they became unhappy, or did these harsh tones contribute to their unhappiness? Who knows? What we do know is that if you don't drop your guns and ammunition, you'll never end your battles. To find out if harsh tones are reverberating in your house, why not conduct an experiment. The next time you and your mate have a conflict discussion, turn on a tape recorder. Try to forget that the tape is running and speak naturally. Then, listen to yourselves afterwards, and honestly examine how you both sound. I bet you will be surprised. To quote from the poem, "The Louse," by Robert Burns, "O wad some Power the giftie gie us to see oursels as ithers see us." In order to achieve relationship harmony, we must amend the quote in the following way: "To hear ourselves as others hear us."

Requests versus Reproaches

When a woman hurls reproaches at her partner, he doesn't know how to translate her complaints into a request for behavioral change. Take a look at some of the complaints that many women utter:

"You don't love me anymore."
"There's no romance anymore."
"Your work is more important than I am."
"I'm not special to you any longer."

112

Can you see how these complaints leave a man clueless? He knows that he is accused of failing in some way, but such reproaches leave him in the dark. Instead of criticizing and complaining to your partner about what he does *not* do, you must learn to *directly* ask for what you need, before he has the chance to let you down. Make it a request instead of a reproach.

Again and again I have heard unhappy women swear to me that they have clearly told their partners what they need and that their partners simply refuse to respond. Those same blank-faced men swear that they have never heard their wives or girlfriends tell them what they want from them. Is someone lying? The woman has said what's bothering her, and she's said it over and over. So, why hasn't her partner heard her? The answer to the mystery lies in the fact that *most women complain bitterly and forcefully about what they're not getting from their partners.* In the face of heated complaints, a man slips into ANS arousal and his brain literally shuts off. He can't hear or process communications, so it turns out he wasn't lying when he said that he never heard what his wife or girlfriend wanted. The man's lack of hearing makes a woman turn up the volume on her complaints. Big mistake, because, as you know, raising the emotional level further cranks up a man's ANS arousal, and turns him stone-deaf. Take, for example, Mike and Erica.

For years Erica raged over her husband's coming home late, his avoiding her by hiding out in the basement, and his not sharing in household tasks. She cried to me in session that he didn't care for her. I asked her if she had ever explained to her husband how his behavior made her feel. She swore to having repeat-

113

edly told him over the years.

We decided to meet with her husband, Mike, who skulked into the session, like a kid on the brink of a scolding. He sat on my couch and stared at the carpet. Erica told him that she was through with him. She was tired of his lack of responsiveness.

I asked her to stop tirading, and to calmly describe his behavior and the effect it had on her.

She persisted that telling him was useless.

I told her, even if it was useless, to do so anyway. And, this is when the miracle occurred.

She calmly and clearly described the behavior that was troubling her and reported how it made her feel.

Mike suddenly broke into tears and said that he had no idea what he was doing to her. He said that he loved her and would change his behavior. They sobbed in each other's arms and connected for the first time in over a decade.

The upshot of the story is that, thanks to Erica's cool presentation, Mike finally heard her, and he changed his behavior. The couple ended treatment with me soon after. Bad for business, but good for the marriage!

Because of past failed attempts, you may be skeptical or afraid to hope that your partner could actually respond to you. Let's run a little experiment. Directly tell your mate what you want. In order to protect yourself from disappointment, assume that he will not respond. I think you will be surprised at his willingness to respond, assuming that you have a mate that wants a relationship with you and isn't too riddled with Old Scars.

Timing

An important trick for keeping a conflict discussion cool is knowing when to approach your mate. I have often observed that women in unhappy relationships have a knack for approaching their partners at the world's worst times. One woman in my study always cornered her husband for their serious discussions when he was glued to the television set, ready for the big play. He was ready for the "wide receiver," not to receive her. If your mate seems tired, irritable, or preoccupied, abort your mission for another time.

In order to get out of the habit of picking wrong times, you need to Knock Before Entering instead of crashing into your mate like a Mac truck. (We will thoroughly discuss this skill in chapter 10.) The point to keep in mind is that Knocking is a simple process in which you ask your mate, "Is now a good time?" or "Do you have a minute?" These sentences show your consideration for your mate and foster a more receptive response. Knocking also models for your mate how he must use consideration when approaching you.

Wait until the Dust Has Settled

Don't approach your mate in the heat of the moment. Until you are more effective at handling your conflicts, you are in danger of losing your cool and resorting to Fight Traps. So take five, or however long you need, to analyze what is happening for you. Privately examine what Old Scars have been torn open by your current conflict.

Know When to Call Back the Troops

When a discussion seems to be cycling out of control, women in happy relationships know how to do one of two things: abort for a later time, as we have discussed, or use the methods outlined in this chapter to cool the climate down.

Humor

Research shows that anger and humor cannot coexist because the biochemicals that accompany humor are incompatible with those that accompany anger. Humor is best directed at oneself or at a situation, and should never be used at the other mate's expense.

Humor Directed at Self

Beth and Leon were visiting his sisters in Europe. Beth was much younger than Leon, and his eldest sister never missed an opportunity to belittle her in a foreign language that sounded like alphabet soup to Beth. On one occasion, her sister-in-law pulled a high chair to the table and motioned for Beth to take her seat. Beth was fuming, but not being fluent in her sister-in-law's language, she had no choice but to swallow her feelings. Later, when she was alone with Leon, she told him how she felt about his not telling his sister that she was out of line.

"I was very angry at you for not sticking up for me."

"I should have. I honest to God was so caught up in my conversation with Enrique that I didn't see or hear what she did. What do you expect from such an old husband. I'm practically blind and deaf."

"Very funny. O.K. Since you're so old and I'm so young, how about I arrive for breakfast in Pampers tomorrow?"

"And I'll roll in on my wheelchair."

In the above example, humor was used to deflate a situation that could easily have caught fire.

Just Say No to Sarcasm

Humor should not be confused with sarcasm—a potent Fight Trap that occurs when a person pretends to agree when he really doesn't. Sarcasm can also take the form of cutting remarks. If you want to achieve relationship harmony, all forms of sarcasm must be eliminated. Let's replay the dialogue of our couple on European holiday and show how easily their humor could have dissolved into sarcasm.

> *"What happened to your mouth back there?"*
> *"What do you mean?"*
> *"Why didn't you stick up for me. How ball-less can you be?"*
> *"You know how ball-less I am. You've been wearing mine for years."*

Create a Cool Climate
by Meeting Each Other's Needs

In addition to the previous Cool-Down techniques for troubled times, you will also need to master the following techniques, which will help you to insure a cool climate all the time.

Platinum Rule

Most distressed couples live according to the Golden Rule (Do unto others as you would have them do unto you). They behave as though they were attached to each other by umbilical cords and bestow on each other what they, themselves, want. For example, a wife who wants more nurturing may pour affection on her mate, who, in turn, may feel smothered by her acts of love. In such cases, neither partner is fulfilled. Here's another

117

example.

> *Emily wants to be pampered when she is sick;
> while Aaron wants to be left alone when he's under the
> weather. Whenever Aron is sick, Emily dotes on him,
> bringing him soup and medicine, secretly hoping that
> he will get the hint and pamper her when she's sick.
> All her fussing only annoys Aaron. Emily needs to stop
> giving Aaron what she needs and to give him what he
> needs, and vice versa.*

In happy relationships, spouses recognize each other's separateness, and live by the Platinum Rule (Do unto the other mate what you know he or she wants).

Acceptance of Differences

In happy relationships, both partners are willing to tolerate differences on many levels. In unhappy unions, divergent opinions and attitudes are taken as personal insults. In order for a marriage to thrive, partners must be secure enough to recognize and allow each other to exist as separate beings.

It is vital that partners tolerate each other's feelings and emotions as well, which rarely happens in distressed relationships.

Don't Mind Read

On a related note, since men are accustomed to taking matters in their own hands, they often assume what their partners want and need, and act upon their assumptions, without checking. These assumptions can easily lead to broken hearts. For example, when Blain and Tamara separated, Tamara moved back with her parents. The couple visited each other on weekends, hoping to achieve a reconciliation. For weeks Blain faithfully visited his wife, until he learned that, after their visits, his mother-in-law harped on her daughter about how much she disliked him.

In order to spare his wife the pain of her mother's nagging, he stopped visiting. His pulling back was his way of caring for his wife. Only one problem: she didn't want him to stop visiting and felt rejected by his withdrawal.

Distressed partners get into trouble when they assume what their mates think, feel, and need and then act upon these assumption. The spouse on the receiving end of these "gifts" often feels wiped out and rejected. So, in consideration of your mutual separateness, and in order to avoid relationship distress, never assume what your mate needs. Always check.

No Unilateral Decisions

One way to turn the relationship climate into the sweltering tropics is to make decisions that affect your partner, without mutual discussion. Make sure that you talk over every plan, big and small, before making them a reality.

Paul and Claire had accumulated forty thousand dollars in their savings. One day, without consulting with Claire, Paul emptied the savings account in exchange for a 380 Mercedes. He was floored to find that his wife was in tears. "But, Paul," she sobbed, "you just blew the down payment for our house."

Remember the Weekly Special

In addition to the broad suggestion that couples maintain a five-to-one ratio of positive versus negative communications, my research has shown that, in order to feel loved, a woman requires frequent reminders that she is special to her husband.

Husbands often tell me, "I show her that she's special. I come home on time. I don't cheat. I give her my paycheck." In response, wives say, "Every good husband contributes in this way to his family. It is an obligation. A duty. I need to know what is special about me? Why you care for me instead of someone else." In short, women need regular reminders that they are as special to their partners today as they were in the first days of their relationship.

Giving flowers and chocolates has become the industry standard way of showing wives and girlfriends that they are loved. The only problem with flowers and chocolates is their universality (all men give them); and, hence, some women feel that a husband who bears flowers is performing a ritual rather than expressing a true feeling of love. This predicament can be easily solved: simply communicate to your mate what actions or gestures he can perform that would make you feel special. A phone call, a massage, a weekly date, buying you a piece of jewelry, preparing your favorite meal. You may be thinking, "But I have told him a thousand times what I want." I must remind you again that most women make two fatal mistakes: They either complain over what they are not receiving, thereby rendering their partners deaf and unresponsive; or they make general rather than specific requests such as, "Treat me special," instead of saying, "I would feel special if you would surprise me with a new dress."

Believe me when I tell you, if you clearly communicate your needs, without being vague or critical, a loving partner will usually respond favorably.

The men I have worked with have found it helpful when their partners create a Weekly Special list from which they can freely choose. The key word here is free: Men must feel free to choose how they will demonstrate their love to their partners. So the list must not read like a series of commands.

Also, it is important for men to understand that women feel loved and cherished when their mates initiate loving gestures, without prodding. If a woman feels that she must beg, plead, or remind her mate to deliver the Weekly Special, she will feel deeply hurt or burning mad. Since the only burning we want to see are the flames of love, remember that the Weekly Specials need to be initiated from the heart and without reminders.

Hamburger Helpers

For those of you who are unfamiliar with Hamburger Helper, it is a packaged food product designed to turn minute quantities of leftover meat into a complete meal, thereby making a little go a long way. One day, the idea struck me: women need relational Hamburger Helpers. That is, in addition to the Weekly Special, which is a loving action, women need regular verbal reminders that they are near and dear to their mans' hearts.

Don't Forget His Pat on the Back

In order to help your mate respond to your needs without being nagged, a pat on the back for his efforts goes a long way. Never forget that while women need to be reminded that they are special, men need verbal reminders that their efforts are appreciated. So, make sure to let your mate know that you value his efforts to respond to your needs, and tell him every day.

Meeting Your Mate's Needs

In unhappy relationships, both partners fight to insure that their individual needs are met. In happy unions, partners focus on meeting each other's needs. In doing so, you become a source of pleasure and healing, rather than a source of frustration to your mate. Harville Hendrix's book, *Getting the Love You Want*, describes how devoting yourself to your partner's needs will result in the satisfaction of your own needs. I highly recommend this book.

Conveying Emotional Understanding

The feeling of being understood (Perceived Understanding) is considered by some marital researchers as the most important element in a happy relationship. It is an especially difficult skill for men to acquire, since they think in action-oriented terms, and find it hard to believe that understanding alone is often all that is required. The best way to teach this skill is through gentle guidance during a discussion. The following is an example of how to do this.

> *Ethel: My sister was so mean to me. What did I ever do to her?*
>
> *Jim: I have good mind to call her up and give her a piece of mind. (fixing, action-oriented.)*
>
> *Ethel: I know you mean to be helpful, but what would help me most right now is your simply listening to how I feel. (gentle guidance)*
>
> *Jim: What good is that? I think you'd feel better if you called her back and gave her a piece of your mind. (fixing, action-oriented)*
>
> *Ethel: Honey, I know you want to fix this for me. Just understanding how I feel is all the fixing I need." (again, gentle guidance)*
>
> *Jim: You mean if I listen to you and understand, you'll be happy?*
>
> *Ethel: That's all I need.*

Keeping Promises

Broken promises are hurtful and damaging to a relationship. When a partner habitually breaks promises, we can suspect that a passive aggressive personality disorder—in which anger is expressed indirectly by breaking promises or withholding—is operating. Broken promises can also result from a dependent personality disorder. The dependent partner will make promises that he doesn't wish to keep, simply to appease the other spouse or avoid the other's anger. When broken promises are caused by character disorders, professional help is in order.

There are also occasions in which broken promises are not caused by personality disorders. For example, men often follow a course of action which they think will please their partners, and in so doing, they often forget or override previously made promises. It has been observed that men find it difficult to simultaneously pursue two courses of action.

Louis had promised to take Tina to dinner to celebrate their tenth anniversary. Earlier that week Tina found a house that she fell in love with. From that moment on, Louis made it his sole priority to find a way to buy her that house (goal-oriented), and he spent every waking hour looking for a way to finance it. Unfortunately, he forgot that he had invited his wife for a dinner date. When the time of the date came and went, Tina was crushed that he had forgotten her. From Louis's point of view, he was thinking of Tina, and only Tina, but this obliterated from his memory his scheduled dinner date with her.

Tina found some solace in understanding the way Louis's brain is wired. He forgot their dinner date, because his brain had a hard time simultaneously processing the two

123

imperatives, the house purchase and the dinner. Broken promises damage trust and erode relationships. It is important to do whatever is needed to follow-through on commitments.

Verbal Embraces

When a man finds it impossible to respond, in action, to his partner's request, he can still respond with verbal open arms. I always use the following example to demonstrate my point.

Judy was in a jewelry store admiring a diamond ring. She said to her husband, Kurt, "I love that ring so much...I wish you could buy it for me." Kurt, in turn, responded in a negative fashion by saying, "What are you crazy...you know we can't afford that ring." This response crushed Judy, and not because he couldn't or wouldn't buy the ring, but because he didn't convey the feeling that he would have loved to buy the ring...if he had the money. By saying, "I would love to buy it for you...it would look so beautiful on you. I am so sad that I can't afford to give it to you now. As soon as I can, you know I will," he would be conveying his wish to say yes to her feeling or wish, even though he couldn't respond in action. Saying yes to a woman's desires is often just as fulfilling as consummating the wish.

Seeing the World From Your Mate's Point of View: Partial Identification

The Cool-Down techniques described above will remain a cumbersome list of directives that are easily forgotten, unless you develop partial identification—that is, a place in your heart and mind for your partner. Partial Identification is nothing more than knowing how to keep one foot on your mate's emotional side of the fence. No relationship can thrive without it.

I do not suggest that you forget who you are and become a clone of your partner. That would be total identification. Total identification is sometimes experienced when two or more persons obtain total similarity of opinion or feelings. This state may occur during a concert or at a religious ceremony of unusual intensity. Total identification is not always a plus. It occurred during the political rallies organized by the Nazis, when participants experienced such enthusiasm that their individuality disappeared in the common excitement. Partners, at times, can also reach nearly total identification—also called merger. In these cases, the separateness of each person disappears and the couple lives under the illusion that they are in total agreement on ideas, opinions, and emotions. For some couples, this merger is an ongoing experience. For others, it is only transitory: during great sex or while strolling together on moonlit ocean boardwalk. These privileged moments of fusion are efficient ways of maintaining and re-creating the unity of the marriage. Although these moments may create the illusion of permanent and total unity, such unity does not exist as a permanent reality. It is broken when the separateness and differences reappear in the daily activities. And, when this illusion of unity is broken, conflict often develops.

Some couples experience conflict because they perpetually live in a state of merger. Merger leads to mind reading; and when this occurs, partners believe that they know what the other needs, wishes or feels, and invariably fail to recognize each other as separate beings; hence, they are inattentive to each other's real needs.

What is desirable in marriage is the conscious joining of two persons who, in spite of their differences, work to combine these differences through mutual understanding. This unity of two different persons is the achievement that

125

causes both partners to feel that their individuality is acknowledged, respected, and understood. It is reached through Partial Identification, which means that you remain yourself, stay in touch with your own needs and agendas, but make space in your heart and mind for your mate's needs and feelings.

Partial Identification is most easy to achieve when the two interacting people are similar; when they share the same culture, life experiences, values, or moral codes. Twins can readily identify with each other. Similarity of gender also helps. We all know the camaraderie that exists between soldiers, club members, fathers, husbands, etc. Similarly, women have their cliques, clubs, and coffee klatches.

More difficult, is Partial Identification with members of the opposite sex, even when they share much in common in terms of culture, social class, or religion. This is why spouses commonly complain about the opposite sex. In the film *My Fair Lady*, professor Higgins exclaims: "Why can't a woman be more like a man?" And women, sipping their coffee, make fun of their obtuse husbands who do not grasp the simplest aspects of female psychology.

The difficulty in understanding someone of the opposite sex is usually compounded by other differences (ethnic origin, religion, culture, social status, tastes, interests, etc.). In spite of all these differences, people who desire a happy relationship, must work at understanding each other, that is, they must Partially Identify with each other.

Interestingly, when you are engrossed in a book, play or movie, you often actively identify with the characters, which can help you better understand yourself and your mate. But, obviously, you also need to discover your partner directly; to determine how you both are similar and how you differ. Daily dialogue, mutual openness, patient description of points of view are necessary to discover what feelings each of you experience in given moments.

This basic groundwork is necessary and must be undertaken before any conflict or tension can be successfully addressed. If you practice Partial Identification during moments of calm, the skill will be firmly under your psychological belt when you need it most: when a tension erupts. But, make no mistake, no matter how much you have practiced, when trouble hits, you will find it very difficult to partially identify. However difficult it may be when you are confronted by your partner, you must temporarily put between parentheses your own ideas, opinions, or emotions and make space in your mind and heart for those of your partner. If you succeed, your Partial Identification will express itself in sentences like: "I see what you mean" or "Yes, I can understand that you felt x, y or z when I did this, or when I said that."

For the process to be successful, you must resist the temptation to defend yourself; you must also be willing to accept responsibility for the fact that your behavior or words have created discomfort, pain, hurt, or anger in your mate.

In order to understand what your mate feels and take responsibility for your part in creating that pain you must be sufficiently secure of your worth. You must possess a solid self-esteem.

To help yourself accept your relational shortcomings another condition must be met. You must realize that it is not possible for your partner to accept and identify with globally negative statements. This is why global accusations, insults, and name-calling (Fight Traps) are the enemies of relationship happiness. For example, "You did it again."; "You will always be the same bastard (or the same bitch)."; "You never show me love and respect" are all difficult to accept due to their globality. Expecting the attacked partner to identify with these across-the-board condemnations would be tantamount to requesting that person to commit psychological suicide. Similarly, the attacked partner may be tempted to use sarcastic self-deprecations, under the pretext of identifying with his angry mate. ("Yes, you are right, I'm an abominable husband. Yes, I understand, I'm a beast, utterly stupid, an sob.. etc.") When such sarcastic answers are made to an accusing partner, they cannot be sincere or express any form of identification because, who in his right mind could identify with such statements about himself?

In order for the confronted partner to partially identify with his mate's statements or feelings, the confrontation must be limited to a specific aspect of behavior. For example, a statement like "When you used the word x, y, or z, I felt very hurt" is an acceptable confrontation that permits the confronted partner—through further questioning—to understand the feelings that his/her behavior created.

In essence, it is the responsibility of the confronting partner to construct a precise and focused description of the problem and to present it coolly. In so doing, the person who is on the receiving end will find it easier to partially identify with what is being said.

You need to also realize that, during a successful conflict discussion, Partial Identification is practiced by both partners. The confronting partner has two tasks: he/she must speak in a way that the mate can tolerate and must also be able to Partially Identify with his or her mate's reactions to the confrontation. And the confronted partner must Partially Identify with the feelings that his or her mate presents. So, as you can see, both partners need to Partially Identify with each other.

How can you learn to Partially Identify with your mate? You both must open your hearts to each other and tap into your feelings of love. I can't stress this point enough: love is the key that unlocks your heart and permits you to Partially

Identify with each other.

How can you access feelings of love when you are angry? A good way to do so is to recall those special moments together, those rare periods of total identification that I spoke of before. You may recall a particularly excellent sexual encounter; you might choose to recall one of your partner's qualities that you especially love. Whatever works for you.

Exercises to Partially Identify with Your Mate's Feelings

Exercise One

In addition to accessing your feelings of love, another way to perfect your Partial Identification skills is to temporarily switch roles. Select an area of conflict and play your mate's position, and vice versa. Make sure to play your roles believably. Feel the way you know your mate feels; state your mate's position. If you have played your part well, you will have an easier time empathizing with your mate's emotions. And, if you make the effort to mentally switch roles when conflicts arise in the future, you will be taking a giant step toward resolution.

Exercise Two

Sometimes, it is difficult to partially identify because you are having a hard time relating to why your mate feels the way he does. To get around this, forget the situation that triggered his feelings, and, instead, recall an instance in which you felt what he feels. Once you have the feelings in mind, you can more easily understand your mate, even if you can't relate to the specific event that triggered his emotions.

♡♡♡

By applying the various Cool-Down and Partial Identification techniques described above, you will abort your partner's ANS arousal and withdrawal behaviors. The result of this is a mate who sticks around to resolve conflicts with you.

Now that you know how to cool the relationship climate, you are ready to move into the second part of the book, which will show you how to resolve your conflicts. The first chapter in this section outlines the one skill that is the bedrock of conflict resolution: listening.

8

Listening to the Battle Cry: How to Use Your Ears to Resolve Conflicts

On the road to conflict resolution, listening is the superhighway. The need to be heard is no idle need; it is deeply healing to the soul and the mortar of a happy relationship. This explains why women in unhappy relationships most frequently complain that their partners are unable to properly hear and respond to their emotions.

In this chapter, I present the Listening Blunders, the enemies of good listening that must be avoided at all costs, and outline the Listening Blocks that cause them. I also describe the five basic listening skills and show you how to teach your partner to be a good listener.

Why is Listening So Necessary?

Each time there is a social unit of more than one person, it is essential that the parties properly communicate. And, of course, no communication is possible without mutual listening. To be happily united, partners must learn a special kind of communication—emotional communication—and a type of listening—listening to the emotions. While you must listen to your boyfriend's or husband's emotions in order to prevent ANS arousal, it is perhaps even more important that your partner learn to listen to yours. This is because relationship satisfaction is highly correlated to a *man's* ability to listen to his partner.

Feeling heard and understood is so vital to a woman's

satisfaction in her relationship, that there is actually a technical term for it: Perceived Understanding. As a consequence, this chapter will concentrate on the type of listening that is most crucial to relationship satisfaction: listening to each other's emotions and, more particularly, teaching your partner to listen to yours.

Because your partner has not been socialized to listen to emotional communications, he will need to do the lion's share of learning. Being less skilled than you puts him in a one-down position, which is a hard place for a man to find himself. So be sensitive to his feelings of vulnerability and be careful not to make him feel patronized.

Also keep in mind that you and your mate may become frustrated by the time required to master listening skills; when you are ready to give up, remember that emotional listening is not something that can be learned overnight, so don't put a stopwatch on the listening learning curve. You must keep practicing the exercises contained in this chapter in order to reap the benefits. Listening skills take time to acquire.

Before I show you the various listening skills, you must first identify and eliminate the Listening Blunders that occur when listeners unwittingly drop their mates. The Blunders fall into two categories: Blunders of Inattention, and Blunders that Break the Emotional Connection. Let's start with Blunders of Inattention.

Don't Hang Up, I'm Still Talking

In Don't Hang Up, the listener ends the conversation without checking to be sure that the speaker is finished. This makes the speaker feel emotionally dropped.

Yvonne: I was so sad today.

Hank: What about?

Yvonne My friend, Sara, is moving to Texas next fall.

Hank: That's a bitch. What's for dinner?

In the above example, Mike started out with a bang, but ended with "dinner." Many listeners forget to make sure that their partners are finished before they "hang up" the discussion. A simple, "Are you finished?" or "Would you like to stay with this a little more?" or "Can we move on?" is all that is required.

I'll Get Back to You

In I'll Get Back To You, the listener drops the speaker with the intention of returning to the topic. Unfortunately, the speaker has no way of knowing that the listener will ever return, not at least in this century.

Denise: I was aggravated today when your mother called and told me off.

Frank: What about?

Denise: She said that I should be spending more time at home with you and the kids.

Frank: It's really none of her business. Which reminds me, my boss's line was tapped and they taped him propositioning a hooker, can you believe it?

Denise: What does that have to do with what we were talking about?

Frank: I was going to come back to it, but when you mentioned mom's phone call, it reminded me of the boss.

In the above example, Frank broke focus with Denise,

leaving her to feel dropped and unheard. A listener should never shift the topic of discussion before the speaker is finished. If this must be done, then it should be done explicitly (like call waiting), so that the speaker knows that the listener will be returning.

Changing the Subject

Changing the Subject occurs when the listener abruptly alters the topic of discussion.

Kathy: The bus was late today.
Neil: My boss was sick.

While Changing the Subject can reflect inattention or a skill deficit, it can also have the effect of breaking an emotional connection, the second type of Listening Blunders, which I will discuss next.

You're Sucking Me Dry

This Listening Blunder occurs when the listener makes a self-referential, nonconnecting response to the speaker's emotional communication. For instance, a wife says to her husband, "I just remembered our anniversary celebration, and a wave of love came over me." To which the husband might reply, "Yes, I felt so happy that day." This answer is an emotional remembrance, not an emotional response. By referring to his own inner feelings and not linking back to his wife (for example, he could have said, "I still feel the same love for you"), she will feel emotionally dropped.

Another, subtler example of a self-referential response is the following. A wife says, "I have very loving feeling towards you," and the husband replies, "What *you* just said makes me feel very happy." At first glance, the response provides the illusion of connection, because the husband made an explicit reference to his wife, using the word, "you." But, his sentence only addressed his own contentment. Like a child, the husband is happy because his "mommy" has fed him emotionally. But where does this leave the wife? With chafed nipples!

What was missing in this husband's response was an emotional communication that echoed his wife's feeling statement. Something like "I feel happy and close to *you* when *you* tell me that" would be in order.

Changing Emotional Levels

Changing the Emotional Level is a gross form of nonlistening that occurs when the listener shifts the conversation away from an emotional content. It occurs regularly in intimate relationships and invariably leads to conflict. It I discuss the reasons why many men Change Emotional Levels under the heading, "Fear of Intimacy," which is in the next section on Listening Blocks. For now, let me simply show you some examples of changing emotional levels.

In the following example, Burt changes emotional levels with an abrupt escape.

Anne: I feel so happy that you're my husband...
Burt: Thanks. How many years have we been married?
I need to know for the insurance.

In addition to an abrupt escape, a person can also use subtler tactics to avoid an emotional connection.

Jeff and Donna, are getting dressed for a night out with friends. Donna catches a glimpse of her husband knotting a necktie he hasn't worn since their honeymoon. "Oh Jeff," she says. "I remember the first time you wore that tie. We were dancing at the Lido di Venezia.. I can still feel your arms around me. Just looking at you wearing it makes me feel so much love for you."

A subtle way to blow off such an emotional connection would be for Jeff to offer an intellectual comment. "Yes, it's an old tie. The type of pattern they used in the nineties."

Jeff could also avoid connection by saying, "Yes, it's a nice tie. Do you remember where you bought it?" In this case, there is a seeming connection—the recognition that the tie was a gift from Donna—but the connection is factual, not emotional.

Not Leading With the Feeling

Not Leading With the Feeling occurs when the listener provides an unemotional response to the speaker's feeling statement.

Laura, an attractive blond with blue eyes that were pink as an albino rabbit's, thanks to nonstop crying, was desperate because she could never connect with her husband. Every time she made a feeling statement, he answered by talking about stocks. She discussed the matter with him and thought he had understood.

"But, last Saturday night was another example," she said. "The kids were away at the sitter's house and we were at our favorite restaurant, Chez Marcel. It was very romantic, candlelight, soft music... Anyway, I could tell women were giving David the eye. He looked so cute. So, I smiled at him and said, 'you look so handsome tonight. You're getting me turned on.' And then he did what he always does. He started talking

about his office and my heart turned to ice. I wanted to crawl in a corner and die."

When Laura confronted David, he answered: "I was about to tell you that, today, a client saw your photo in my office and said how pretty you are."

As you can see, David's heart was in the right place but his words were in the wrong order. He didn't lead with a feeling statement, which would have connected to Laura.

Rushing in With Solutions

Offering practical solutions is another way of bypassing a woman's emotional communications. When a man jumps to offer solutions, he means to convey that he understands his partner's problem; unfortunately, the opposite is achieved, and the woman feels emotionally dropped. In order for a woman to feel heard, her partner must verbally convey that he understands her feelings and leave it at that. See the section on Male Listening Blocks, under the heading "The Doer Freaks," to understand the cause of this blunder.

Cheer Up

When a man tells his upset girlfriend or wife to Cheer Up, she feels stifled and angry. This angry reaction totally bewilders men. (Why is she so mad? I'm trying to comfort her.) If your partner employs the Cheer Up Blunder, he needs to be told that if he wants you to cheer you up for real, he must ride the storm out with you—meaning, accept your feelings and stay on your emotional level for as long as you need.

What Causes Listening Blunders?

Now that you are familiar with the various types of Listeners

137

Blunders, you need to understand and resolve their causes.

The Blunders of Inattention, which occur when the listener is preoccupied, can be due to three different factors: skills deficits; intense preoccupation; and/or fear of asserting oneself.

When Listening Blunders are due to skills deficits, they can be easily remedied by becoming aware of the Blunder and practicing a better response.

If intense preoccupation is causing the Listening Blunders, you both will need to become more aware of your inner states, so that you can directly communicate when you are unavailable to listen, rather than listen with half an ear. What's more, the speaker can protect herself from being on the receiving end of this type of blunder by making sure that her mate is available to listen to her before she launches into an emotional discussion.

The third cause of Blunders of Inattention can be due to what I call the Unentitled Citizen Syndrome. In such cases, the listener is afraid to assert himself and tell his partner that he is not available for discussion; so, he will pretend to listen— saying, "Uh, huh, yeah...," while continuing to pursue his own line of thought; and in the process, he may commit any or all of the Listening Blunders. Before someone can be a good listener, he must first entitle himself to defer a discussion politely when he isn't 100 percent available to listen.

The Blunders of Inattention are generally not the result of deep-seated Listening Blocks. However, the second type of Listening Blunders—refusal or avoidance of emotional connection—can be caused by various types of blocks, which I will discuss in detail below. Keep in mind that some Listening Blocks are unique to men, others to women, and some are shared by both sexes. I will begin by discussing the Listening Blocks that are common to both sexes.

Listening Blocks

Discomfort Over One's Own Feelings

If a person is unable to tolerate the strong feelings that are induced by the speaker's communication, it will be impossible to listen and properly respond.

The next three Blocks—Poor Self Control, Applying Laws of Morality to Feelings, and Applying Laws of Logic to Feelings—all stem from the discomfort that arises when strong feelings are discussed. These blocks also involve an unconscious attempt to push down intolerable feelings.

Poor Self-Control

Since listening automatically stirs feelings in the listener, when a person believes that all feelings must be acted upon, then the only way to guard against going out of control is to avoid feelings and the listening that triggers them. Sexual and aggressive impulses are particularly threatening because of the consequences that would result if they were to be enacted. That's why I call these two impulses the Dynamic Duo.

Theresa entered my office hanging her head in shame. She told me that she could never divulge to me what she was feeling because I wouldn't like her anymore. I wrote down on a piece of paper all the "horrible" feelings I could imagine and asked her to circle all that applied. Big surprise. Sex and anger were circled.

Why couldn't Theresa openly admit to her feelings? Because she fears that her behavior isn't fully under control. If she feels like axing her husband or having sex with the mailman, then she must act the feeling out, right? Wrong. You can think and feel whatever you want, so long as you know that you can separate thoughts and feelings from actions. Once you've got it straight, feelings have lost all their power. Until this Block is resolved, it will be impossible to listen to each other's feelings.

Applying Laws of Morality to Feelings

When someone feels that it is morally wrong to harbor negative feelings, that person will indict either himself or herself whenever unacceptable feelings surface. The person suffering from this problem, will often be heard saying," I (You) shouldn't feel that way" or "I (You) have no right to feel that way."

Condemnation of feelings makes it hard for either partner to stay on the other mate's emotional level, in which case, listening will go out the window.

Concepts such as "right" or "wrong" have no place in the emotional realm. Feelings cannot be squelched by moral preachings.

Applying Laws of Logic to Feelings

Many people try to reason away their feelings ("It doesn't make sense to feel the way I do," etc.). Since feelings are as irrational as the wind, applying laws of logic to the emotional realm is an exercise in futility. Imagine saying to the wind, "It would be better if you blew from the opposite direction!" In order to be good listeners, both partners must be able to accept all their feelings.

Inability to Identify With Your Mate

Another Listening Block occurs when your mate finds it

impossible to understand how and why you feel the way you do. When this occurs, your mate is having trouble identifying with you. And, in this case, the tendency is to pull away emotionally or to say things like, "I don't understand why you're so upset." Obviously, these remarks let the speaker know, loud and clear, that her mate is not able to hear her.

If inability to identify is either your or your mate's problem, refer again to the Partial Identification exercises, which are thoroughly described in the previous chapter.

Fear of Intimacy

Since the listening process creates a close bond, if a person is terrified to be too close, that person will have a tendency to tune out emotionally laden communications. Fear of intimacy often conceals a fear of dependency, abandonment, engulfment (self-annihilation), etc. Refer to chapter 5 on Old Scars in order to find out how to heal these wounds. Until these Old Scars are resolved, Listening Blocks will continue.

Male Listening Blocks

Feeling Responsible

As I've said before, since men feel responsible for their partners' well being, when a woman is upset, her partner tends to feel guilty. In order to assuage his guilt, he will attempt to fix the problem by trying to talk her out of her painful feelings (the Cheer Up Listening Blunder). When a man is engaged in this operation, listening goes down the drain.

The Doer Freaks

Since men have been socialized to be fixers, not feelers, they find it hard to stew in the emotional juice with their wives. For them, any conversation about feelings is a waste of energy and time—meaning, the conversation needs to end as soon as possible. As a consequence, men will pull out their psychic toolboxes and try to fix their partners' problems with the only gadgets they have: rationalization, intellectualization, and, most of all, problem-solving. These men do to their partners exactly what they have been trained to do for themselves—to reroute their feelings into the intellectual and practical realms, where they can be extinguished by solutions. This rerouting, of course, takes them miles away from listening.

You can turn your partner's practical/logical tendencies to your advantage and to the advantage of your relationship by methodically teaching him the various tasks and skills associated with effective listening. In this way, his productive side will be satisfied.

The Macho Defense

Many men are terrified to let down their macho guard, fearing that their maleness will be lost. (They feel that their sexual apparatus may shrivel and fall off if they are not acting like "real men" every minute.) "Sitting with" a woman who feels upset, forces a man to confront his own feelings of vulnerability. To help your Wimp Phobic get around this block, remind him that "It takes a tough man to make a tender...listener."

Female Listening Blocks

Fear

When your partner is finally willing to acquire listening skills, you may discover mindsets in yourself that threaten to jam the wheels of progress. In chapter 2, I explained that many fears keep us from moving ahead. No one is telling you to give up your fear, but it would be best to move forward in action (listen to your partner), despite the feeling.

Anger

If you have felt unheard for a long time, you may be resistant to listen to your mate. ("He never listened to me, so why should I listen to him?") Acting on this feeling is an emotional payback—a Fight Trap—that you need to lose.

To soften your resentment, remind yourself why your partner hasn't been listening to you—he's been in chronic ANS arousal. This should help you to extinguish your resentment and start listening to him. When you listen, you will be heard in turn, and your anger will soon subside.

Also keep in mind that holding on to your anger will interfere with your husband's listening abilities. If you are seething with rage, you risk communicating inappropriately. In order to be heard, you must make sure to communicate a message that's "hearable." This means that your verbal communications must not be attacking or critical, otherwise ANS arousal and withdrawal reactions will be triggered in your mate, the very reactions that interfere with his listening abilities.

When I speak of a message that's hearable, I am referring to more than overt verbal content. Recent studies have shown that nonverbal behavior can also trigger ANS arousal and withdrawal behaviors in men who are in distressed relationships. Nonverbal behaviors include body language (facial and bodily expressions), gestures, and vocal tones. Keep in mind that a mean look or a harsh or whining tone of voice is all that is required to set off that downward chemical spiral that ultimately leads to male withdrawal. So it's entirely up to you whether or not you will speak and behave in a way that makes your mate want to unplug his ears.

I Won't Praise Him

If you want your partner to learn to listen to you, you need to praise his efforts. Many women greet this suggestion with the enthusiasm reserved for a dental cleaning. They often tell me, "He should have known how to listen all along." And where was he supposed to learn listening skills? In school? From his father?

Why is it that women freely praise their girlfriends but are reluctant to praise their husbands' learning efforts? There are several reasons for this. The first one is chronic resentment. When you feel angry, words of praise don't naturally fall from your lips. But there's deeper reason for the reluctance. It stems from the belief that a husband should know what you need without your having to tell him what you want, let alone praise him. To explain where this expectation comes from, we need to understand the preverbal stage of childhood. Since a young child cannot speak, he or she requires a parent who is capable of sensing every need. If the parent succeeds in properly guessing, great. If the parent doesn't, which is usually the case, the child is left with a craving for a correction. Cut to twenty years later: we marry and our unconscious minds see a second chance to receive the emotional goodies we weren't fortunate enough to receive as kids. This explains why, when a wife is furious that her husband doesn't magically know what she needs, she is really saying, "My mother should have guessed what I needed and you owe it to me to make up for my earlier losses."

Heaven knows it's hard enough for a biological mother to guess correctly each and every time. How on earth can a husband, a male who was never trained to be emotionally tuned-in, be expected to guess. But, this is what many wives expect, and when their husbands do not guess or guess wrong or don't even realize there is something to guess, they are furious. So, when a woman refuses to praise her mate, she is actually thinking, "He didn't give me what I want, so to heck with giving him praise." Talk about shooting yourself in the emotional foot.

In order to get past this impasse, you must remind yourself that your mate cannot be a mind reader. What's more, humans cannot acquire new behaviors if praise is withheld. When you praise his efforts, he will be motivated to engage in the hard work necessary to learn the listening skills that speak to your heart. So you will actually be doing yourself the favor.

Now that you have identified your Listening Blunders and are working on resolving the Blocks that cause them, you are ready to learn to listen.

Listening Defined

As we embark on our emotional listening crash course, the first thing you need to know is that listening is an active process that requires two separate tasks: (1) *clarifying* that the speaker's statements have been accurately perceived; and (2) *verbally conveying* to the speaker that the delivered message has been heard and understood.

I underscore the word *convey*, because it is common for a man to silently reflect on his partner's communications, but offer no response. As far as a woman is concerned, she might as well be talking to a gerbil. In truth, many men, if asked to do so, could probably accurately restate the essence of their partners' communications (presuming they aren't in cognitive shutdown). But a woman doesn't know that her partner "got it" unless he tells her so. I cannot stress strongly enough that effective listening is actually effective responding.

Listening Skills Translated into a Man's Language

Since men are most at ease in the logical and practical realms, their willingness to acquire listening skills increases when they are presented as task-oriented steps. Nearly every husband or boyfriend who has followed my program has learned to listen and respond to his wife's or girlfriend's emotional communications. As Karl told me, "I always loved Gina, but now I have the tools to listen, and she finally feels how much I love her."

Put a Sock in it and Just Listen

In order to teach your mate to listen to your feelings, he must get the idea that he needs to put a sock in it when it comes to offering unsolicited advice or solutions. Of course, you can't tell him in these words, but you can tell him, in concrete terms, exactly what you do need from him. When I say, "Be concrete," I mean spell out exactly what you expect from him. Remember, psychics know how to read minds, so if you need him to listen and stow the solutions, then tell him.

Dottie, like many women, assumed that her husband knew that she needed him to simply listen to her when she was upset. So, when Russell gave her advice instead, she figured he was just being a withholding bastard. (Remember how our minds can be our own worst enemies.) By believing this, Dottie set herself and her husband up for war. Whenever her husband pulled out the advice, she pulled out her weapons of destruction. Not surprisingly, when she started firing, he had no idea why. When Dottie was finally able to tell Russell, in concrete terms, that he should skip the advice and simply listen, he started to get the picture.

Based upon my research with all types of couples, the following phrase most effectively gets the "put a sock in it" point across: "I know you mean to be helpful with the advice, but what would really help me is if you would just listen and understand what I'm feeling."

Becoming a Good Listener: Five Basic Skills

There are five basic skills that people who are successful listeners employ in combination. These are: Mirroring; Restating; Asking for More; Questioning to Clarify; and Staying on the Same Emotional Level.

Mirroring is nothing more than reflecting back exactly what the other person has said. This technique shows that a person is listening. Restating is a form of Mirroring in which the speaker's message is *reworded slightly.*

Asking for More is a technique in which the listener draws out additional information.

Questioning to Clarify insures that the listener has thoroughly understood the speaker. This questioning process serves two purposes: it clears up any confusion that may exist, and it shows that the listener is actively listening.

Staying on the Same Emotional Level helps the speaker feel psychologically held, heard, and understood.

Let's start with Mirroring.

Mirroring

Exercise

Choose a subject that is bothering you, but make sure to avoid your hot topics. We don't want intense emotions to interfere with learning the technique. Now, *coolly* discuss one feeling that has been aroused in you as a result of your conflictual issue. It is your partner's job to mirror back the feeling that you present. When his Mirroring is accurate, you will say, "Yes." If his Mirroring is inaccurate, try again until he succeeds. Then, move on to your next feeling. It is a good idea for the listener who is Mirroring to use a questioning vocal inflection. In this way, he leaves room for you, the speaker, to clarify in the event of misunderstanding. Use the following dialogue between Amy and Ken as an example of how you can practice Mirroring.

> *Amy: I can't believe that my boss didn't say hello to me today.*
> *Ken: You can't believe that he didn't say hello?*
> *Amy: Yes. And it really hurt my feelings.*
> *Ken: Your feelings were really hurt?*
> *Amy: Yes. And I even felt a little nervous that my job may be on the line.*
> *Ken: You're worried that your job may be on the line?*
> *Amy: Yes.*

You get the idea. This exercise is driving home a technique that good listeners use automatically. Whenever a person's words are mirrored back, it creates the feeling of being truly heard.

Restating

In the next exercise, Mirroring is elaborated upon through Restating. Restating is an excellent skill because the speaker knows that someone is making an attempt to understand, rather than just mimicking, which, if used to excess, can make the speaker feel like she is talking with Polly the parrot.

Exercise

Amy: I can't believe that my boss didn't say hello to me today.
Ken: You were surprised, weren't you?
Amy: Yes. And it really hurt my feelings.
Ken: Besides surprised, you felt hurt too?
Amy: Yes. And, I even felt a little nervous that my job may be on the line.
Ken: So, you were surprised, hurt, and nervous all at the same time?
Joan: Yes.

Asking For More

Asking for More information serves a clarifying function and conveys that someone is making an active attempt to understand. This technique is achieved by combining interested body language (raised eyebrows, wide eyes, and nods) with words like "And?" or "And then what happened?" The following passage shows how it works. The best way to teach your partner this technique is for you to demonstrate it for him.

Liz: You know my sister was really nasty today.
Gene: What did she do this time?
Liz: It was the tone of her voice. She was really snotty.
Gene (leaning closer, eyes widening): What did she say?
Liz: She told me that because I hadn't been working for a while, that I wouldn't understand the competitive-

149

ness in her office.
Gene: And what did you say?
Liz: I told her that I was offended....
Gene: And then what happened?...

I think you can see how effective this technique is in conveying interest in all the details of a mate's communication.

Questioning to Clarify

Researchers have found that happy couples live in harmony because the men in these relationships possess excellent encoding skills—meaning that they accurately interpret what their partners say. Make no mistake, good encoders are not psychics by birth. In fact, these men probably are as much in the dark as distressed boyfriends and husbands when it comes to understanding what their partners mean when they speak. So how does a happily united man manage to interpret his partner properly? It happens through a questioning process. Developing this skill takes practice, but it's worth the effort to learn; this is an essential listening skill. The following dialogue shows how Questioning to Clarify looks.

Pauline: You know, I can't believe that you had to be late for dinner so many times this week!
Tim: Are you saying that you're angry with me about it?
Pauline: Well, I am angry, but I don't think that I'm angry with you.
Tim: Well, then who are you angry with?
Pauline: I'm pissed with that job of yours.
Tim: That job is putting food on the table!

150

Pauline: I think that you're feeling attacked by me.

Tim: Yeah. I was starting to get a little hot.

Pauline: Let me start over. I appreciate what a good provider you are. I'm just annoyed that your boss makes you work late so often.

Tim: So, you're pissed at my boss?

Pauline: Yes. And, I wanted you to just understand that when you're not here I really miss you.

Tim: So, you miss me, eh?

Pauline: That's it, mainly. And, I hope that boss hires the assistant he promised soon.

Tim: I miss you too, you know. Anything else?

Pauline: Come home earlier as soon as you can!

Tim: You know that I will. And, I understand how hard it is on you and the kids.

Questioning to Clarify—The Five Questions

To develop the Questioning to Clarify skill, deliver a feeling statement and have your mate ask five clarifying questions. For example:

Opening statement: I was really upset today.

Question #1: Did I do something? (Questioning rather than jumping to conclusions)

Clarifying statement: Not at all.

Question #2: If it wasn't me, then who upset you?

Clarifying statement: I really need a few minutes to calm down.

Question #3: Are you telling me to leave you alone? (Not jumping to conclusions. Checking before acting upon a potentially wrong interpretation)

Clarifying statement: No, don't go. Maybe you could give me a hug and comfort me.

151

*Question #4: Sure. When you say "and comfort me"...
was there something besides the hug that would
comfort you?*
*Clarifying Statement: Yeah, a massage would be nice
after a hug.*
Question #5: A massage and a hug and that's it?
Clarifying statement: That would be great.

Had the husband in the above example not asked the
five clarifying questions, he could have easily misinterpreted
his wife's communication. What's worse, misinterpretations
often turn to disaster, because many husbands act upon their
false assumptions. I can't stress enough the relationship-sav-
ing importance of learning the Questioning to Clarify process
along with the Five Questions techniques.

Looping Back Until Consensus is Reached

If the Questioning to Clarify process were to be dia-
grammed it would appear as large loops, and loops within
loops. The loops indicate questions, clarification, restatements,
and more requests for clarification. This process is continued
until "perceptual consensus" or a meeting of the minds, is
reached. Here is an example of Looping Back:

"I'm really sick of these family vacations."
*"Are you saying that you don't want to vacation with
my family anymore?"*
*"I wouldn't go that far. It would be nice if we didn't
vacation with your family every summer."*
*"So you don't want to vacation with them every sum-
mer?"*
"Right. Maybe every other summer would be better."
"So it sounds like every other summer would suit you.

But, I'm wondering...since you said, 'Maybe,' are you not entirely sure?"

"It's true. I'm not sure.. If it's OK with you, can we leave it open and can talk about it when next summer rolls around?"

"O.K. We'll discuss it next summer."

Staying on the Same Emotional Level

Staying on the Same Emotional Level is a listening skill that is the exact opposite of the Listening Blunder, Changing Emotional Levels. Staying on the Same Emotional Level means that, for the duration of your listening process, you consciously become the Siamese twin of your mate. As a twin, you don't try to pull left or right; to do so would create psychological injury similar to the tearing that would occur if you tried to pull the twins apart. Staying on the same emotional level is a form of Partial Identification.

The best way to teach your spouse how to stay on your emotional level, is to forewarn him, before you begin speaking, that the communication you are about to deliver is of an emotional nature. By alerting him before the discussion begins, you will help to abort his natural tendency to shift the conversation away from feelings and onto solutions. It is preferable to put him in the right frame of mind before the talk begins, rather than wait until he fails. Reproaching him for his failure to stay on your level is the best way to trigger ANS arousal, which will make it impossible for him to listen to you in any form.

Ten Minutes a Day Keeps the Marriage Counselor Away

Now that you and your partner are familiar with basic listening skills, what comes next? Let's start with ten minutes of One-to-One Time per day, in which you take the time to listen to each other. At first, you should be the only speaker, and your partner the listener. I say this because it is too overwhelming for a man to learn to listen to his partner and disclose his own feelings at the same time. After your mate has successfully mastered the skill of listening to your feelings, you can include another ten minutes for him to discuss his own, if he wishes. Don't be surprised, however, if he isn't chomping at the bit to disclose feelings about issues that are bothering him. Most men prefer to concentrate on solutions that they devise on their own. So your partner may want to spend his ten minutes explaining how he resolved a problem.

Before you begin your ten minute One-to-One Time, remind your partner that he is to listen and not offer advice or try to talk you out of your feelings.

Keep it Light For Starters

Don't start by discussing the topics that concern your partner's behavior toward you. They are too hot, and until you have learned how to properly handle these delicate subjects (discussed in the following chapters), you must practice in more neutral territory. It will be much easier for your mate to listen to you when he doesn't feel personally responsible for having caused your ill feelings. So, for starters, discuss an issue that has nothing to do with him at all. Once he is able to successfully hear your feelings on a neutral subject and has some success under his belt, then you can move into deeper relationship waters. Examples of subjects to start with: someone who annoyed you at work, on the road, at the bank— your best friend, your boss, your mother, father, sister, brother. I repeat: stay away from your mate and the relationship.

Time and Place

Set a time and a place for your One-to-One Time. The only way that this "date" can be broken is if one of you is dead! Also remember not to have this discussion in the bedroom. I don't want you to associate heavy conversations with the bedroom. Heavy breathing, yes; heavy conversations, no.

Strokes

After you have completed your discussion and your mate has succeeded in listening, praise him to the hilt. Remember that it is human nature to want to repeat pleasurable experiences. If your mate recalls that your talk time was positive and that he succeeded, he will be ready to take on the next listening challenge.

And, don't be too discouraged if you had to remind your mate to keep his advice on hold; reminders are normal in the beginning. In any case, your mate deserves praise for hanging in there and trying to listen.

Ten Minutes a Day Keeps the Marriage Counselor Away—Part 2

After your partner has managed to listen and stay cool during several ten minute rounds, you are ready to discuss a relationship issue that is upsetting you. Since I don't want intense emotions to gum the works, please save the hottest relationship topics for later, after you have mastered the techniques in the last chapters. Above all, avoid issues that are close to your mate's ego, such as sexual performance or anything else that you know to be a hot topic.

In fact, while you are learning the listening skills, I suggest that you discuss a make-believe problem. If you and your mate are hardcore realists and must discuss actual issues, make sure to present neutral issues (for example, behaviors that are upsetting you but that can be easily remedied). Only you can say what qualifies as a relatively neutral issue for you both.

♡ ♡ ♡

The listening skills that I have discussed in this chapter are the bedrock of successful relationship communication. When practicing your listening skills, it would be helpful for you to conceptualize the skills as notes in a musical scale. By artfully blending the various notes, you too can compose relationship harmony.

While I focused in this chapter on helping boyfriends and husbands to build listening skills, you also need to perfect yours as well. As you read the next chapters, you will see that listening skills are required at each phase of conflict resolution. If you do not listen to your partner, your discussions will derail long before you see a resolution. Only keen listening will enable you to recognize when a discussion is derailing, bring it back on track, and see it through to resolution.

9

On Furlough: Knowing When Not to Negotiate

Before you learn to negotiate, you need to know that, in many instances, negotiation is not required and may even be inadvisable. I know you may be thinking that I am complicating matters. But, in the end, I will actually be saving you a lot of headaches.

Many relationship manuals and therapists are quick to advise distressed couples to negotiate because it is a structured process that yields observable results (when successful). But there is another reason why people are quick to negotiate: it helps them to avoid feelings.

We all know how uncomfortable emotions can be, and so it feels easier to negotiate a contract—an agreement that outlines behavioral change—and steer clear of emotionally rough seas. In the short run, everyone feels better, but in the long run, the tide of emotions swell even higher. This is because the overt issues have been negotiated, but the underlying emotions still churn beneath the surface. And when this happens, your negotiations will fail and you will feel even angrier than before.

There are other reasons why negotiations may fail: you may be negotiating nonnegotiable issues. There are three classes of issues that are nonnegotiable: violations of what I call Relationship Laws; Emotional States; and Value Conflicts. Let's examine these in detail.

Violations of Relationship Laws

There are basic requirements that must be met in order for a relationship to survive, and whatever people think or say, if these are not obeyed, there is no relationship. Here is a list of these violations.

Degrading language, name calling, sarcastic put-downs

Physical abuse of the partner or the children

Sexual abuse (partner or spousal rape, sexual abuse of the children)

Infidelity (unless both partners have agreed to an open relationship or marriage)

Alcoholism/drug abuse

Irresponsible spending behavior or gambling that endangers the welfare of the family or impinges on the other partner's needs

Refusal to discuss and arrive at agreements regarding parental practices

Refusal to work (job or housework) and equitably support the family

Systematic refusal to consider partner's or spouse's feelings and to work at understanding them. (example: "That's the way it is. If you don't like it, the door is open.")

If you are the object of any of the above behaviors, you must put your foot down and state that they are unacceptable. A mate's systematic and repeated refusal to change is cause for separation, not negotiation.

At this extreme point, couples often make one last-ditch effort and schedule an appointment with a marriage counselor.

However, the rigid disposition of either of the partners may render this last ditch effort dead on departure.

Emotional States

Emotions that are triggered by your mate's actions or words are the second class of nonnegotiable issues. Let's say you feel hurt that your husband forgot your birthday this year. How can you negotiate about being hurt? The birthday has passed. All that is left are your feelings, which need to be heard and understood, not negotiated. I insist on this point because many couples will try to negotiate their feelings away.

> *Ron: Susie, you know life would be easier if you didn't get so angry each time I make a joke about your weight.*
> *Susie: Are you trying to tell me I shouldn't feel the way I do?*
> *Ron: Yeah, kind of. I'd be more willing to work around the house, if you didn't get so upset with me.*

While you can negotiate about behaviors that upset you, the feelings that arise out of your mate's upsetting behavior cannot be negotiated or bartered away. So, when dealing with your own emotional states, the best way of operating is to disclose your feelings, and for your mate to listen and understand, using the techniques discussed in the last chapter.

A good way to help your mate understand your reaction to his words or actions is to use the Should I Be Feeling...? technique. This technique helps a fragile or defensive partner discover the effect that he has had on you, without your having to point the finger at him. For example, you and your mate are discussing a subject—the content doesn't matter—when

159

suddenly he blurts out, "You don't know what you're talking about." Your feelings are wounded, and you need to help him understand how his words landed with you. Obviously, you can't negotiate a contract about your emotional reaction to his words. And if you blast him outright for his inappropriate behavior, he will probably become defensive and tune you out. Here's where the Should I Be Feeling...? formula comes in handy. You would say, "Should I be feeling"; then, you would insert your feeling—whatever it may be. In the case of the above example, you would say, "Should I be feeling put down?"

The advantage of this technique is that it helps your mate discover the impact of his behavior (enhances his Partial Identification) without getting his back up. Be aware, however, that some highly defensive mates could respond to the formula by saying, "Feel however you want to feel. Your reaction has nothing to do with me." In such instances, the mate is refusing to look at himself and accept responsibility for the effect of his words or actions; in these cases, you will need to use a variant of the above technique, and, instead of saying, "Should I be feeling, x, y, or z," you would say, "How do want me to feel when you talk to me that way?" This question forces the other person to take a look at his behavior.

Not only are your emotional states nonnegotiable, the same holds true for those of your partner. Again, I have to distinguish between feelings and actions or reactions. That is, if your mate acts on his feelings and behaves inappropriately, that behavior can be negotiable. But the feelings themselves—that is, the raw emotions—are not fit for negotiation.

Eleanor's husband, Michael, often freezes up when she approaches him for an emotional connection. On one such occasion, she put her arms around him and told him that she had just remembered one of their first dates, in which they danced cheek to cheek at an elegant nightclub. Michael was silent and unresponsive and stared into space. Eleanor was crushed and fled the room, in tears.

Why did Michael freeze up? To find out, Eleanor needs to approach Michael and explore the origin of his reaction. In doing so, she will discover that his action-oriented brain had mistakenly translated her communication into a request that he do something concrete—to take her to the club in the near future. Michael knew that they didn't have the money for a night out, and he became immobilized by the fear of disappointing her.

In a situation like this, there is no place for negotiation. Michael can't negotiate on fear; and, he can't negotiate about his wrong interpretation of his wife's request (thinking that she wants to go dancing) because this has nothing to do with what she expects of him—an emotional connection. Negotiating about dancing would play into Michael's action-oriented tendency, and it wouldn't address what the conflict is about: the fear that was aroused in him when he mistakenly translated her request for connection into a request for action. What Michael actually needs is to focus off of actions and learn to talk about his own feelings and respond to his wife's.

Even though your partner's emotional states cannot be negotiated, you may find it helpful to negotiate what is called an Interpretive Contract. This is an oral contract that focuses on the circumstances that may give rise to intense emotions and/or cooperating with your partner to abort particularly severe emotional reactions. With this type of contract, one partner is given permission to point out—without recriminations— troublesome or hurtful behaviors when they occur, or to spark a mate's awareness before a habitual reaction has the chance to occur. For example, Eleanor and Michael's Interpretive Contract might be the following: Michael gives Eleanor permission to warn him before she attempts to make an emotional connection (to head off a freeze-up). She will also remind him that no action (or expenditures) are linked to her upcoming approach, to help him take the focus off of action. And Michael agrees to clarify the nature of her request, in order to do what he can to head off his immobilizing fear. The discussion that is inherent to an interpretive contract will teach Michael to be less action-oriented because when thoughts and feelings are put into words they are much less likely to be enacted. And what's more, the intense emotions that cause him to freeze up will also diminish, thanks to the cathartic nature of the talking process.

If you and your partner decide to engage in an Interpretive Contract, there are two points to keep in mind: (1) You must make sure that your partner consents to having his frailties pointed out. Without his consent, you risk offending him, which will only trigger ANS arousal and we'll be back to square one again and; (2) When you spark your partner's awareness, you must do so in a loving way. He must get the feeling that you're working on this problem as a team. If, at any point, your mate feels mocked or belittled, this technique will prove ineffective and even counterproductive.

Value Conflicts: Nonnegotiable

Value Conflicts are the third type of nonnegotiable issues. When I speak of values I am referring to religious, cultural, or political beliefs, tastes, preferences, and so on. These values make up the core of an individual and are not up for negotiation. To attempt to do so would be like trying to force a leopard to change its spots.

There is much to be said for homogamy—or similarity—of values in intimate relationships. In fact, homogamy is highly correlated with relationship satisfaction: there is little friction, since the couple already sees eye to eye. Couples who are less homogamous, but still get along, have learned to either accept their differences or steer clear of conflictual subjects.

Unfortunately, many distressed couples are in trouble because they are fighting about and negotiating value conflicts, without knowing it. For example, you and your mate have different preferences regarding where you like to have sex: Your mate wants sex on the living-room floor, whereas, for you, the Beautyrest mattress is as wild as you like to get. Neither person's preferred location is wrong. Each of you is entitled to his or her tastes.

On the subject of tastes, let's discuss Vicky, whose bathtub drain is clogged beyond belief with a lethal-sized hairball. "If only Pete would outgrow his hippie phase and buzz saw that mound of spaghetti on his head, I wouldn't be forced to play Mrs. Plumber," she lamented to me. She went on to explain that Pete likes his hair long and refuses to cut it, and they habitually argue on this subject.

Is this a negotiable issue? It's about Pete's hair values, and either Vicky can live with them or she can't. However, if Pete's long hair impinges on her by clogging the drain, then she may have a subject worthy of negotiation.

We have spoken so far about the fact that attitudes, tastes, and preferences are nonnegotiable, but what about habits? If habits are value laden, then they are also nonnegotiable. For example, each Saturday morning, you like to dive into the household chores, but during that time, your husband has a habit of lounging on the couch, avoiding anything productive. You may feel tempted to negotiate for a change of behavior.

163

But, what if your husband's habit is value laden? Let's say he was raised an Orthodox Jew and was prohibited to do any work on the Sabbath. In this case, relaxing on Saturday mornings is part of his value system.

Here's another example. A husband has a habit of paying the bills at the very last minute. He was raised by parents who were hippies. They believed that life should be primarily fun and freedom filled, and that work and chores could be done whenever. So as you can see, this husband's habit of paying bills in the eleventh hour is also value laden.

Now, if his wife was raised in a family that taught her to be early for appointments and deadlines, then, her expectation that the bills be paid early is also value laden. In this case, the couple has a clash of values. What can be done about this?

Since values are an integral part of a person's makeup, you can't ask someone to negotiate away a part of his identity anymore than you can be asked to do this. Demanding that your partner alter a behavior that is value laden is like asking him to commit psychological suicide. What's more, expecting someone to relinquish a value laden behavior is tantamount to saying that his value is wrong and yours is right. This type of qualitative judgment doesn't apply to values. Values may clash but they can't be labeled wrong or right.

So how can you deal with a value conflict? You have three options: (1) Ask yourself, "Do I really want to get into a war over this value-laden habit?" Asking this question may lead you to simply accept your differences; (2) You can address the value conflict as though it were an emotional issue by listening to each other's points of view, without trying to enforce a behavioral change on each other; and (3) As a result of your mutual understanding and respect for each other's values, you may decide to negotiate a resolution that is acceptable to you both, one in which both your values are respected. To do this, follow the negotiation steps outlined in the next chapter.

When dealing with habits that annoy you, it would be wise to ask yourself, "Is this habit directed against me?" Since women are prone to excessive personalization, you need to beware of the tendency to wrongly assume that your partner is hanging on to a habit to intentionally annoy, provoke, or defy you. Ask yourself, "Would my mate still engage in this annoying habit if he lived alone?" Did he act this way before I was on the scene?" Very often, when you examine the issue with a cool eye, you will realize that the habit is not directed against you. This may help you to let the issue go.

Sometimes, value conflicts are smoke screens for deeper issues. For example, Paula and Jerry continually argue about whether to marry or not. He believes that love is all that counts and that a piece of paper is not needed to prove his love. Paula wants a complete wedding bash. These two people share different values on the subject of marriage. Either they can decide to live with their differences or they can't. But, there also may be more going on here than meets the eye. Maybe Paula and Jerry are fighting about "I do" or "I don't" instead of facing deeper issues. Perhaps fighting about whether to marry or not conceals deep fears of intimacy and commitment.

Beware the Tendency to Negotiate on the Overt Fight Content

Many couples in marital counseling are guided to negotiate on overt subjects of conflict; but the contracts that result from these negotiations often don't work because the couples never addressed their real conflict—that is, the feelings underlying their overt issue. Since emotions can be so painful, the mind will often cut off from the feelings and focus on behaviors. For example, instead of admitting to yourself that you feel hurt and frightened when your mate comes home late, you may be inclined to confront him on his various actions. Why didn't he call? What was he doing? Who was he with? Once you veer off onto a discussion of behaviors, the natural progression is to negotiate a contract that outlines more acceptable behaviors. It sounds good on paper. But the feelings of fear, hurt, and anger were not addressed. They have gone underground, and will reappear in another form at another time. Hence, negotiating won't resolve the true issue—the feeling of insecurity and anger. When negotiation proves ineffective in solving an area of conflict, you must always assume that feelings were brushed under the emotional rug.

Lilly was hurt and angry that her partner never pitched in to help her around the house. For years the couple worked in therapy and negotiated numerous contracts, to no avail. When Lilly came to see me she bemoaned the fact that her partner didn't care. I quickly realized why contracting had never worked for this couple. Her partner had not understood how she felt about handling it all. Lilly had been the Cinderella of her family of origin and was forced to do all the work while her sister lounged on the couch. Lilly had unconsciously re-created her family of origin and no amount of contracting was going to take this problem away. She needed to realize first what Old Scar she was trying to heal through her repetitive fights. Then she had to decide to relinquish her old role as Cinderella. Once she reached this level of realization and resolution, she could explain to her partner how his behavior made her feel and resolve this impasse.

I hope you now understand why the emotions that underlie your conflictual issues must be addressed before you can even think about negotiating. But here's where things get a little tricky. Beneath the feelings that we are aware of lurk even deeper feelings that we may not know. And if you want to resolve your conflicts, you will need to go beyond the overt emotional layer, and access what I call your Emotional Core—the deepest part of yourself. Unless you unearth your core feelings, you will have little hope of resolving your conflicts. In order to help you do this, in the following section, I detail situations that commonly arise in relationships and help you identify the core feelings that are likely to be aroused in each case.

Where Were You? Who Were You With?

When you find yourself interrogating your mate, the overt feelings that accompany your third degree are jealousy or anger. But the obsession that your husband is out with someone else can conceal a core fear of abandonment.

You Always Take His or Her Side over Mine

When your partner sides against you—by aligning with one of your children or with his parents, undermines your rules, or bribes the kids with money or treats, your overt feeling is anger. But the core feeling are likely to be hurt and a sense of betrayal.

You Don't Give Me Enough Money

When you aren't given enough money either because your partner is stingy or he spends the money on himself and his toys, your overt reaction is probably anger over being unconsidered. Your pocket may be empty, but your heart is even emptier.

And your core feeling is that of being unloved.

You're Sinking Our Financial Ship

When your mate spends excessively, empties the savings account, charges the credit cards to the max, or is erratic in paying bills, your overt emotional reactions may be anger and outrage, feelings of powerlessness, a sense of being out of control, abandoned, and betrayed. But the core feeling in this case is terror for your life.

You Don't Give Me Enough Sex
(or the Right Kind of Sex)

When you feel deprived in the sex department, the overt reaction is often hurt or anger. A feeling of rejection often lurks beneath; and even deeper may be the feeling that you are starving for love.

You Don't Let Me In

When you feel emotionally shut out by your mate, the overt reaction is often anger, loneliness, and hurt. And beneath these feelings may be a core feeling of insecurity or a core fear of abandonment.

Honey Pass the Beer, and Don't Block the TV Screen

If your partner doesn't lift a finger around the house, or lounges while you are doing all the chores and/or childcare, you will probably feel used and angry. On the core level, you may feel demeaned and worthless.

You Don't Spend Enough Time With Me and/or the Kids

When your mate places his life, his business, his hobbies, or his friends ahead of you and the children, you may feel hurt and angry on the overt level. On the core emotional level you will probably feel rejected and worthless.

You Don't Tell Me You Love Me
If you feel deprived of verbal affection, you will probably feel hurt and angry on the overt emotional level. But this issue may conceal an even deeper feeling of worthlessness.

What Happened to the Wine and Roses?
If your partner has stopped romancing you, you will probably feel, hurt, neglected, and angry. But, at your core you probably feel unloved, unwanted, and also worthless.

You're Not My Father
When your mate controls you, you will probably be aware of feeling angry and defiant. On the core level, you may actually be feeling inadequate and devalued.

There are many reasons why I encourage you to access the core feelings that lurk beneath your overt emotional reactions. For one thing, when your emotional toes have been stomped on, the initial reaction is usually anger. Even if you don't act on that anger, your partner may still view you as a witch on wheels; and you know what will happen then. By contrast, when you reach inside yourself and access your deeper emotions—the feelings that are beneath the anger—and communicate them to your mate, there is often an instant shift in him: faced with your Emotional Core, his own feelings of love, empathy, and caring will be naturally aroused. And then, one of two outcomes usually occurs: Either he will alter his behavior spontaneously; or he will be more willing to negotiate a modification.

This is why embarking on a negotiation before your mate understands the emotional significance an issue holds for you will lead to a poor outcome. Without this understanding, your request for a behavioral change will make him feel resentful, as if he's being forced to yield just because you want him to. What you want is a willing change, not a forced change.

♡♡♡

To sum up this chapter, I have presented three classes of nonnegotiable issues: violations of Relationship Laws, Value Conflicts, and Emotional States.

Violations of Relationship Laws simply need to be stopped, not negotiated.

Value Conflicts are nonnegotiable; however, the behaviors that arise out of these conflicts may or may not be negotiable. And as I have said, the emotions that are stirred as a result of differing values can certainly be handled in the same way that you will address your Emotional States.

If you believe that you are dealing with a negotiable issue, I still suggest that you address the Emotional States surrounding your issue first, following the recommendations in this chapter and the chapter that follows.

The mere fact of opening your heart and truthfully sharing the impact of your mate's behavior may be sufficient to stop the upsetting behavior, in which case you will be able to stop short of a full-scale negotiation. This is often true, but there will be occasions in which your partner may still be resistant to changing his actions. When you are dealing with entrenched behaviors such as bad habits, disagreements over the division of household chores or childcare tasks, the allocation of money, or other similar conflicts, negotiation may be the only answer.

10

The Peace Treaty: How to Negotiate a Contract

Y ou are now ready to learn how to negotiate a contract. Years of research has proven to me that how you introduce your subject of conflict is key to a successful outcome. If your issue is not properly introduced, your partner will be gone before you can get past the starting gate, let alone make it to the finish line.

Why Do I Have to Do All the Work?

Many women don't object to initiating conflict discussions, so long as their issues are presented in destructive ways, such as laying blame, complaining, criticizing, etc., but when they are asked to be positive and constructive, they balk. ("Why do I have to be the one to change? I'm tired of doing all the work. And, why do I have to be the one to bring up the problems anyway?") You may feel annoyed, but you have to face facts: Women are the relationship watchdogs, which means that we are the ones to notice problems; we are the relationship overseers and maintainers. So, how can a man be expected to initiate a discussion around a problem that he doesn't see?

Keep in mind that your resistance to changing how you address your conflict discussions may conceal a fear of relinquishing your armor of anger. You can continue to do what you've been doing or you can do what works. The choice is yours. If you want to achieve resolution, then the next step is to learn to introduce your problems for discussion in a constructive way.

Getting Started

Let's start with your feelings. Something was said or done that you didn't like. Maybe you felt hurt or angry. Get it into your head that the specific feelings and actions that triggered your reaction don't really matter. I'm not saying that your feelings don't count. The point is that from the point of view of conflict resolution techniques, the issues and feelings are immaterial. The techniques you will be using to communicate your feelings will remain relatively constant.

Self-Work

Before you bring your problem to your mate, you will need to complete some Self-Work tasks that include: identifying the Old Scars that the conflict rekindles; recognizing the Fight Traps you feel like using; Draining Off the emotional venom; Digging Up Love; preparing your Ice Breaker—which announces that a problem exists, the Lead-In—which is a supportive statement, and your Problem Statement; determining whether or not you are dealing with a negotiable issue; and preparing for a full-scale negotiation, if this applies.

After having read the list above, you may have felt tempted to simply bash your mate over the head and skip the Self-Work. I understand the temptation, but where will giving up get you? In jail or out of the relationship. So, for your own sake, don't give up now. Riding a bike seemed daunting at first, as do the Self Work tasks. But once you become familiar with them and practice a bit, the tasks will no longer seem overwhelming. So let's look at these tasks more closely.

173

Identify the Old Scar

Figuring out what Old Scar has been activated by your mate's words or actions will help you redirect your focus away from your partner and onto the ghosts of the past.

You will need to figure out what Old Scars your current fight may have stirred in your mate as well. This information will assist you in creating a Problem Statement that is most suited to your mate's needs. What's more, the better you understand what is happening emotionally for your mate, the more you will be able to keep the discussions on track or steer them back on track when they derail.

Recognize Your Fight Traps

During this next portion of Self-Work, note whatever fears you have about bringing your issue to your mate. Do you fear that your mate will be unreceptive to you? Do you think that your directness will make matters worse? Based upon past disasters, your fear is probably well-founded.

Your fear may also be warning you that your creature-of-habit brain is threatening to rear its ugly head. That is, your unconscious mind may try to trick you into saying or doing things to get your mate riled up so that he (as well as you) will act in the old, familiar ways. So don't write off these fears so fast; they are telling you something very important. And if you are afraid of a bad outcome, be extra careful to recognize and not to play out your old Fight Traps. Remember, falling into Fight Traps may float your boat in the moment, but your relationship will sink in the end.

Drain Off Raw Rage

Lisette was terrified to speak to her husband about

her issue, for fear that he would bite her head off. Soon, Lisette discovered that she was actually afraid of her own anger—she actually wanted to destroy her husband, Scott, verbally. Her holding back was a defense against her secret wish to let herself rip. In order to move past this sticking point, Lisette needed to admit how angry she was with her husband and Drain Off the emotional venom.

Like Lisette, you too will need to Drain Off your rage so that you are as cool as possible when bringing your issue to your mate. A good way for you to do this is to fantasize exactly how you would do your mate in. Do you want to brain him with a frying pan? Or Krazy Glue his lips shut and beat him senseless with a rubber bat? Whatever fantasy you choose is harmless so long as you know that you can't and won't act on it. So, fantasize away and mentally Drain Off all your anger. When you're finished, you will feel emptied out and almost ready to approach your mate with a cool head. But draining off your rage isn't all that's needed. You also need to access your feelings of love.

Dig Up Love

It is difficult to access feelings of love when you are feeling angry with your mate. This is because when you are upset, your mind tends to associate the currently upsetting event with memories of similar instances in which your mate let you down. When this happens, your mind "floods" with bad memories and you find yourself drowning in negative feelings. The only way around this impasse is to consciously stop the flow of negative associations. Once you have stopped yourself from flooding, you need to go one step farther and remind yourself that you are overlooking the good aspects of your relationship and your mate. And once this is done, you are ready to Dig Up Love by recalling memories of special moments with your partner and/or reminding yourself of the qualities you love about him.

After completing these four tasks, you are emotionally ready to move onto the next phase of Self-Work tasks: preparing the wording for your Ice Breaker, Lead-In, and Problem Statement. The goal of this task is to choose words and phrases that you know will open your mate's ears and heart. Let's start with the Ice Breaker.

The Ice Breaker

An Ice Breaker is a sentence that alerts your mate that you need to discuss a problem. I suggest that your Ice Breaker be as neutral as possible (you don't want to be seen as a "you know what" breaker). Ill-worded Ice Breakers such as "We have to talk right now" or "You've done it again," are sure to get your mate's back up; and you can forget the dream of seeing a healthy discussion unfold if his fur is bristling. More preferable are sentences like "I have something that's bothering me. Is this a good time for us to talk?" or "I need your help with something. Do you have some time to talk with me now?" When you deliver the Ice Breaker, make sure that you adopt neutral body language and speak in a cool vocal tone.

The Lead-In

Next, prepare the wording for the Lead-In. The Lead In is a positive statement that puts your mate at ease, guards against ANS arousal, and creates a loving and safe climate for your discussion and/or negotiation. In the Lead-In, you will state why your mate is important to you, what you value about your relationship, or what traits you admire in him. Keying in on traits that will facilitate the upcoming negotiation kills two relationship birds with one stone.

The Lead-In may also include knowledge of self or other. Here you may allude to Old Scars, if you think it would be helpful. Mentioning his Old Scars can convey that you understand why the particular problem you are about to discuss will be painful or difficult to face. For example, you might say, "I know that you were criticized as a kid and that confrontations can be painful for you." By conveying your knowledge of your mate's Old Scars, you are positioning yourself as a friend who wishes to do no harm. Be careful not to wield his Old Scars like a baseball bat, bashing, mocking, or belittling him. For example, statements like "You never grew up" or "You're just like your father" are attacks and do not set the stage for a constructive discussion.

Sample Lead-Ins
"I value our relationship and the love we share..."
"You are very special to me..."
"I have always admired your willingness to face prob-
  lems head on."

When the Lead-In is prepared, move on to creating your Problem Statement.

The Problem Statement

Basic Considerations
The Positive Confrontation
No matter how you sweeten the blow, delivering a Problem Statement is a confrontation. Most distressed couples have mastered the art of negative confrontation, which con-

sists of emotional purging or "getting it off your chest." But, as you know, letting yourself emotionally rip never succeeds and always harms the relationship. So remember, this not the time for emotional venting. You should have already Drained Off the intensity of your feelings during Self-Work, and if you haven't, you shouldn't be addressing your conflict yet.

In fact, you should not approach your mate for discussion until you are ready to provide a positive confrontation that will set the proper climate and make your mate feel worthwhile, at ease, and motivated to want to move deeper into the negotiation process. It is how you present the confrontation that will set the proper climate and determine if your negotiations move forward or not.

Don't Express

As I've told you throughout this book, your chances of resolution will depend upon your ability to stay cool, and this is especially true when you introduce your Problem Statement. Your goal is to *present* what upset you and to *describe*, not express, your emotional reaction. The cooler and more detached you are, the greater your chances for a successful discussion.

One Issue at a Time

When presenting your issue, focus on one problem and only one. Don't forget that many women find it natural to bring up every bothersome issue (the Kitchen Sink Fight Trap), instead of focusing on the one issue at hand. If you throw everything that has upset you since day one, your mate's ANS arousal will kick into high gear, and you know what will happen. So, even if you have several issues to address, remember that Rome wasn't built in a day. We'll get to them all eventually. The key is to not overwhelm your mate by presenting more than one issue. As I often tell women, "Don't bite off more than he can chew."

Don't Respond in the Moment
As a final note, I do not advise you to respond in the moment that you are offended. You risk opening the discussion in a way that is less than ideal. What's more, when you tell your mate what's troubling you, you must be prepared to move directly into a conflict discussion and possible negotiation. And if you haven't taken the time to perform all the Self-Work steps, you won't be ready. So until you are very proficient at resolving your conflicts, I recommend that you wait to talk to him until you have completed all your Self-Work. Now, let's move on to constructing your Problem Statement.

Creating Your Problem Statement
There is a scientifically recognized formula for properly presenting your issue for discussion. The formula is in three parts: first, the Disclaimer; second, the Presentation of Your Issue; and third, the Suggestion for the Future. Let's begin with the Disclaimer.

The Disclaimer
Presenting your problem to a mate whose ego is fragile or eroded (which is the case for most men in a distressed relationship) is a losing proposition. Your partner will feel wounded by the most innocent remarks, and he will resort to making excuses, defending, denying, and counterblaming in an unconscious attempt to pad his psyche. You can't put your problem to someone who must ward off everything you say in order to stay mentally afloat.

Here's where the Disclaimer comes in. It assures your mate that you are on his side, even during a confrontation.

It protects his psyche so that he no longer needs to bandage himself with excuses, defensiveness, and denial. When your mate's ego is insulated, he will be more willing to listen to your issue.

SAMPLE DISCLAIMERS

"I know you didn't mean to hurt (or upset) me."
"I'm sure you didn't realize how you were coming across."
"I know you love me (and the kids) and you don't want to hurt my (our) feelings."

As you can see, the Disclaimer gives your mate the benefit of the doubt. When he feels that you aren't blaming him, he will no longer need to defend himself. If you're still thinking, "My partner knows very well what he's doing to upset me. And giving him the benefit of the doubt would be a flat-out lie" or "I've told him a thousand times what bothers me," remember, you can't say with 100 percent assurance that he ever heard what you said. Until recently, chronic ANS arousal made him deaf to your words.

If you are still skeptical, you have my permission to retain your doubts. In fact, believe, if you like, that the Disclaimer will make no difference. Just use it anyway and watch centuries' worth of wax dissolve from his ears.

Once he is willing to listen, you will be able to present your issue.

Presentation of Your Issue: The X, Y Formula
The proper way to present your issue is using the X,Y Formula, which consists of describing your mate's upsetting behavior and then stating how that behavior made you feel.

("When you do x, I feel y.")

Notice, I told you to focus on the *behavior* that upset you. By focusing on your mate's behavior, rather than on his person, you will be protecting his ego, which will keep his ANS arousal on ice.

It is also possible to reverse the order of the X, Y formula and say, "I felt y, when you said or did x." Based upon what you know about your mate, you will need to decide whether he would respond better if you were to lead with a description of your feelings instead of a description of his upsetting behavior.

Keep in mind that when you say, "I feel," a highly defensive partner may be inclined to throw your words back in your face, "So, that's what you feel. That's your problem, not mine!" The translation of this statement is, "Don't blame me, my ego is too fragile to tolerate being wrong." If your mate exhibits such defensiveness, you can be sure that his ego needs to be handled with kid gloves. And don't be fooled, even if he's a physical Mighty Man, he may actually be an emotional Minnie Mouse. The challenge then becomes how to prevent a fragile partner from blowing an emotional gasket. There is hope. In addition to the deescalating effect of the Disclaimer, there is also another technique that will help your mate swallow your Problem Statement.

AVOID THE WORD YOU

When a fragile person hears, "*You* did x, y or z," he feels that a finger is being pointed at his ego, and you know what that means. You can take his ego off the hook by rewording your X,Y Formula so that the word *you* isn't said at all. For example, "I feel x...when such and such happens" or "I feel x...when such and such is said (or done) to me."

181

Now Prepare the Suggestion for the Future

Your Problem Statement will be complete when you add the Suggestion for the Future. Remember, men feel at a loss to translate your distress signals into concrete solutions. Without your suggestion on how he can improve or please you in the future, he will feel like he's drowning in a sea of complaints. Your Suggestion for the Future appeals to the concrete, goal-oriented side of a man that says, "Tell me what to do and I'll do it."

Devising a clear Suggestion for the Future is a hard skill for many women to acquire, because, as I've said before, it is much easier for us to say what our partners are doing wrong than it is to formulate a clear, concise statement of the behavior we would prefer from our mates.

The inability often stems from a deep-seated resistance to state what we need. This wish is often expressed in sentences like: "If I have to tell my husband what I need, it isn't worth it" or "If he loved me, he'd know what I need." As I said in chapter 8, this wish stems from insufficient or absent mothering early in life. You must remind yourself that no partner can make up for such early deficits. So remember, if you want to stay unhappy, keep hoping that he'll guess your every need. And while you're at it, hope that he will sprout breasts too. You have an equal chance of both things happening.

Another reason why you may find it hard to construct a concise Suggestion for the Future is that, as you know, women have not been socialized to speak in concrete, goal-oriented terms. This explains why you will probably find it easier to say, "Be nice to me" (vague and general) instead of saying, "I would feel special if you asked me out to dinner on Friday night." Or, you might say, "You don't pay any attention to me anymore" (vague, general, critical, complaining) instead of, "I would like you to sit next to me and listen while I talk to you." In order for your Problem Statement to be effective, you will need to speak more like a male and directly state the behavioral change that you are seeking.

Put the Above Steps Together

When all these steps are put together, the way you present your problem to your mate will play something like the following scenario:

Ice Breaker
"Honey, do you have some time to talk with me?"
(You are told yes.)

Lead-In
"I know how hard you have been trying to work with me on resolving our conflicts, and I appreciate your efforts."

The Disclaimer
"I'm sure you didn't realize that I would be upset, but..."

Presentation of Your Issue: the X, Y Formula
"When x is done to me (avoid the word you), I feel y."

Or, you may reverse the order and state the feeling first and the behavioral description second.

"I feel x, when y is said (or done) to me." (Avoid the word you.)

Add the Suggestion for the Future
"But, in the future,
I would feel so happy if you would do or say x."

Planning your words may sound artificial and unspontaneous to you. It is. And I want you to engage in and practice this cumbersome process because it guards against the tendency to blurt out words before considering their effect. We don't want to turn your mate off before discussions have begun.

You still have one final Self-Work task: to determine whether or not you are dealing with a negotiable issue. Remember, Emotional States, Value Conflicts, and violations of Relationship Laws are nonnegotiable. Refer to the previous chapter to refresh your memory on the distinction between negotiable and nonnegotiable issues.

Now that you have completed the Self-Work tasks, you are ready to begin your conflict discussion, starting with the delivery of the Ice Breaker. But before you break the ice, make sure that your mate is available.

Knock Before Entering

If you knock on your mate's psychological door, rather than barging in, your mate will be more responsive to you. An excellent way to knock is to ask, "Do you have a some time for me?" or "Are you busy right now?" If your mate says you may proceed, then deliver your Ice Breaker right away.

After you have delivered a prize-winning Ice Breaker, a couple of things may happen. You may notice a reluctance on your mate's part (more like dread) to agree to talk further with you. Remember, previous "discussions" made him want to run for cover, so realize that if he isn't jumping for joy, it's only past-experience talking. If he seems less than eager to talk, you might say: "Listen, I don't want to rip your head off. I just need your input on a problem."

When you deliver your Ice Breaker, you need to be prepared for the possibility that your mate may not offer you the green light to pursue the matter at this time; in which case, you will need to schedule a discussion for later—ideally during the same day.

You will also be facing a postponement if your mate becomes too defensive to continue. That will require you to reconsider your approach and reapproach at a later time.

If, for whatever reason, your talk has been postponed for later, you both need to schedule an exact time, date, and place (excluding the bedroom or wherever else you have sex).

If your mate says that he would like to talk later, he still may want a clue regarding what you will be discussing down the line. Knowing your mate as you do, you must decide if it is better to give him a hint of what is troubling you, even though you won't be actually discussing the matter until later.

For some men, knowing the nature of the problem in advance of the actual discussion works well. It can provide a feeling of being in control, enable them to digest the initial shock, diminish the fear of the unknown, and even offer an interval of time in which they can begin working on the problem. After all, most men do like to independently solve their problems.

On a related noted, not knowing what will be discussed later can make your partner feel like a kid being called to the principal's office to be reamed out for some unknown offense.

If your mate was often in the doghouse as a child, not telling him what the problem is about and making him wait until later may transform you, in his unconscious mind, into an authority figure. If these associations occur, ANS arousal will be cranked up, and you can kiss your talk good-bye. For such men, alluding to your issue in advance of the actual discussion can be helpful.

The downside of clueing him in to what you will be discussing later is that you may trigger a defensive reaction and have no time to work it through in the moment.

Another danger of giving too much information in advance is that he may become anxious that a confrontation will erupt down the road (especially if your first approach made him hot under the collar), his ANS arousal will mount, and he may be in withdrawal before you get to the bargaining table.

For other spouses, knowing your issue ahead of time can backfire in a big way. So you need to decide whether it would be best to leave the problem vague until the scheduled talk time. If you decide that this is best, merely deflect questions like "What's it all about?" by saying, "Honey, I don't want to rush us. I'll look forward to your input later, when we will have more time." Make sure that you keep the atmosphere light and nonthreatening when you say that; otherwise, your mate will become anxious between now and when you actually sit down to talk. In which case, there will be no talk.

If your mate takes the bait and agrees to talk immediately, then you will deliver your Lead-In and Problem Statement. I remind you again that the Problem Statement opens the door to your conflict discussion and possible negotiations, so you must be sure that all your Self-Work is complete before you deliver your Problem Statement.

You will also need to master the next section before

you deliver your Problem Statement. Otherwise your discussion will be cut off at the knees.

Switching Battle Gear:
Becoming the Discussion Overseer

After you deliver your Problem Statement, be prepared to make an immediate, 180-degree shift in roles from confronter to discussion overseer. Keep in mind that even if you deliver a perfect Problem Statement, your discussion may still jump the tracks. Your job as overseer is to keep a finger on your mate's emotional pulse, watch for signs of ANS arousal, and make sure that your discussion doesn't derail.

Remember to listen and watch the verbal and nonverbal aspects of your partner's behavior. Is he beginning to justify himself (verbal clue)? Is he avoiding eye contact (nonverbal clue)? The following is a quick checklist to refresh your memory on the signs of mounting ANS arousal.

Nonverbal Cues

His voice starts to rise.

He seems overheated (sweating), red in the face, or is breathing heavily.

He is exhibiting early signs of withdrawal behavior: blank, affectless stare, turning away, avoiding eye contact, or he appears to be not hearing, is silent, or looks sullen.

He looks ready to bolt from the room.

Verbal Cues

He has started to justify or defend himself, refuses to

accept responsibility, or makes excuses.
He is counterblaming.
He has begun repeating himself.

If you observe any of the above signs of ANS arousal, you must employ what I call First Aid immediately or else the discussion is going to sour. The goal of your repair efforts is to smooth your mate's ruffled feathers using various Cool-Down or conflict deescalation techniques.

First Aid

Time to Bring Up Ancient History

One way to smooth your mate's ruffling feathers is to Bring up Ancient History. I don't mean that you should dredge up past grievances with your partner, that would only inflame matters more. I mean that it may be helpful to tell your mate what Old Scars have been triggered by your current conflict. This technique is effective for two reasons. It immediately sparks empathy on the part of your mate, because he can see the hurting child in you, and talking about pain that stems from before he was in the picture shifts the focus away from his ego, which aborts ANS arousal and withdrawal reactions.

"When you tell me that we can't ever go out to dinner, no discussion, it reminds me of my dad who never let me tell him my point of view. It made me feel so hurt and frustrated when dad did that to me."

Stress the Hurt Instead of the Anger

Another way to cool down the climate is to focus on your hurt feelings. This should help your mate be more receptive and less defensive.

Cool-Down Questions to Refocus a Mate Who's Losing It
Presuming that your mate's ANS arousal isn't off the charts, the following Cool-Down questions can also be effective in settling him down.

> *"Obviously I am not coming across properly. Can you help me rephrase what I'm saying in a way that would feel better for you?"*
> *"I think that you are feeling attacked by me. This is not my intent. Can you tell me where I'm going wrong?"*
> *"Can you suggest how I could talk to you in a way that won't offend you?"*

There are also the following First Aid techniques, all designed to handle specific discussion meltdowns. The goal in all cases remains the same—to shore up an ego that is fraying in order to arrest ANS arousal.

He Makes Excuses, Defends, or Justifies Himself
When your mate begins to tell you all the reasons why he did what he did, he is obviously feeling blamed or attacked. His ego needs patching or else he'll be out the door any second. Response: "I'm not saying you intentionally set out to hurt (or whatever the feeling is) ...I'm just telling you how I feel" or "I'm just telling you how the behavior landed with me."

When He Says, "But What About My Feelings?"
You, the confronter, should be heard and completely understood before your mate takes his turn to state his own thoughts and feelings. I call this the Emotional Right-of-Way. Distressed partners are so accustomed to not being heard that they have a

hard time waiting their turn. This explains why your boyfriend or husband will demand his own air time before you have finished speaking. ("You feel sad or mad...how do you think I feel?" or "You want me to listen to your feelings, but what about mine?")

When you feel cut-off, your natural reaction will be to interrupt him, which will further contribute to his feeling of not being heard. While you, the confronter, have the Emotional Right-of-Way, you need to keep your eye on the larger goal: saving the negotiation.

You have two ways to proceed at this point: One is to tell your mate: "I am interested in how you feel. Can we finish with me and then get back to you?" The acknowledgment that you are interested in his feelings often helps to bring the discussion back on track. But if it doesn't, you have only one other choice: Deal with his feelings, let him talk, use your learned listening skills, and reflect your understanding of his feelings. When he feels emotionally understood, you should be able to resume the original discussion.

Interrupting

This discussion impasse is similar to the one discussed above. When your partner interrupts you, for whatever reason, you need to know that he is feeling attacked and is on the defensive. Warning bells should go off for you: ANS arousal is mounting. You need to cool things down, and fast. Response: "You have a good point there. Can we agree to get back to it after we finish this?" or, two other alternatives: "I think you are feeling blamed by me...how can I talk to you so you won't feel so upset?" or "Are you interrupting because you aren't feeling heard by me?"

You Shouldn't Feel That Way

As I've said elsewhere, since men feel responsible for their partners' happiness, they also think that it's their job to rescue them when they are upset. And this causes your mate to talk you out of your feelings. ("Let it go" or "It's not a big deal" or "You're being too sensitive.") A good response is, "I know you don't like the feelings in the air. If you listen and understand, my feelings will settle down more quickly."

If you sense that your mate is trying to talk you out of your feelings because he feels guilty for having inflicted pain on you, the following response is ideal: "I think you're feeling guilty and I want you to know that I understand that you didn't mean to hurt me. Just understanding me now will help me feel better."

Counterblaming

Your mate is trying to shore up his ego by saying, "I'm not the bad guy, you make mistakes too." Response: "You have a valid point about me. Could we finish what we're talking about now and get back to what I have done to upset you after we finish this?"

Refusal to Accept Responsibility

When a man's ego is eroded, accepting responsibility for upsetting you is tantamount to admitting that he is a failure. Response: "I know that you didn't mean to hurt (or whatever the feeling is) me when you did x,y, or z. Making a mistake doesn't mean you're all bad. We're just talking about this particular instance." or your might say, "If you accidentally fell on my foot, and broke it, I'd still be in pain. I need you to understand that my feelings were hurt by accident, too."

Another possible block to accepting responsibility

stems from the fear of vulnerability. Your mate may be afraid that his admission of "guilt" will be used against him. If you suspect that this is the case, then the following would apply: "Listen, just because you acknowledge that you did something to hurt me, doesn't mean that I am going to get even or never let you live it down."

Summarizing Self

It has been observed that distressed couples summarize and restate their positions during conflict discussions. When spouses are not feeling heard by each other, they repeat themselves hoping to be finally heard. If you notice that your mate is beginning to repeat himself, it is time to get into high listening gear. And, you better act fast, because not feeling heard is ANS arousal bait. You might say something like, "I notice you have repeated that sentence a couple of times. Did you think that I didn't hear you?" or "Obviously I haven't given you the impression that I have heard and understood what you are saying. Let me repeat what I think you are saying and tell me if I have understood."

If All Else Fails, Abort Mission

If your mate's ANS arousal is off the charts, you may not be able to veer your discussion back on track. If you cannot succeed in cooling things down despite the First Aid techniques described above, then abort your discussion and postpone it until later. Use this interval to analyze where the discussion went wrong. Ask your mate for feedback on what he thinks caused the discussion to derail, using the Cool-Down questions mentioned above. And use your accumulated knowledge to reapproach in a different way.

♡ ♡ ♡

Let's assume that your discussion has progressed smoothly, except for one problem. Your request for change has not been received with open arms, and you are miles away from a resolution of your issue. Where do you go from here?

Time to Negotiate

We are finally ready to discuss those situations in which negotiating a contract is in order. If I asked you to define the goal of negotiation, I bet you would say something like, "to compromise" or to "meet each other half way." You are not alone in assuming that negotiation is synonymous with compromise. In fact, most marriage counselors, pastors, and mediators advise distressed couples to "cut the apple in half"; but, who in his or her right mind wants half the apple? Compromise, by its very nature, leaves both parties unsatisfied and, for this reason, rarely produces the desired results. This probably explains why most couples approach the negotiation process with the enthusiasm reserved for root canal. Well, unclench your teeth. I'm not asking you to compromise. What we are after is collaboration.

Collaboration, by contrast with compromise, is an active process in which both partners put their heads together and devise a creative and unique resolution to their conflict. Even though it takes a bit more effort, you will find that this method produces better negotiation outcomes and greater relationship satisfaction. For these reasons, it is well worth the extra effort.

How to Create a Winning Contract

There are a number of elements that make up a good marital contract.

Be a Friend

In order to negotiate a contract that works, you must be willing to trash your guns and ammunition and address your mate from the perspective of a caring friend.

Be Clear and Specific

To create a winning contract, you will need to clarify the specific details of your contract, including dates, times, places, frequencies, and anything else you can think of. In addition, you will need to make sure that you clearly define the behavioral changes that are outlined in the contract. For example, "I promise to be nice to you" is vague and general. Instead, your contract needs to target specific, observable behaviors. For example, "I promise to take ten minutes each evening to give you my undivided attention."

Outline Positive Changes

If your expected behavioral changes are formulated in a positive, not negative, way, you are both more likely to be satisfied with your contract. Stating what you expect from each other enables you to focus your energies on meeting each other's needs. However, if your contract is framed in the negative sense ("I won't do x") all your attention will be placed on not throwing grenades at each other. While you may reach a cease fire, you won't be meeting each other's needs or resolving your issues.

Manageable Contracts

How many times have you noticed the failure of New Year's resolutions? I will lose 8 million pounds by tomorrow and I will jog 10 thousand miles twice a day. You know how humans set themselves up with unreasonable goals, only to fail. So make sure that the behavioral changes outlined in your contract are small and manageable. You can always expand on the contract in a later negotiation.

The Contract Isn't Carved in Stone

If your contracts are viewed as irrevocable, they will be doomed to failure. For one thing, one or both of you may be reluctant to close the deal for fear that there will be no turning back—especially if the contract doesn't work. A contract should never feel like a life sentence without parole. Don't worry that you're offering your partner a bailout clause. Remember, his previous broken commitments were due to flawed negotiations or chronic ANS arousal, and nothing more.

I Won't Squash You

If your mate was squashed during his formative years, he will unconsciously equate negotiating with "giving in" or "being defeated," which will lead to extremely defensive, uncooperative behavior. Your mate needs to know that you don't intend to shove your agenda down his throat. In giving this message, you become a source of safety, rather than danger. And in this atmosphere, you both can feel safe to negotiate.

Seek Input

The best way to convey that you won't squash your mate is to seek his input on possible solutions. Doing so puts him in the driver seat and sets you up as a friend rather than a controlling parent. You must also beware of a potential setup. If your mate's parent(s) always told him what to do, he may induce you to provide all the suggested solutions. And, if you do so, he may view you as his bossy parent, in which case there is a great danger that he will sabotage the contract. So remember to ask your mate for suggestions on how to resolve your issue. Once all the options are on the table, discuss each one fully. Explore how you both will feel if this, versus that, option is selected. The key here is that you are seeking your mate's input, not shoving orders down an enemy's throat.

Mutuality

In order for your contract to be a success, you must remember one key word: mutuality. If the negotiations are lopsided, and a one-sided contract results, the contract will fail. One-sided contracts leave the person who must do the changing feeling like a scolded child whose parent is forcing him to behave. Resentment and contract sabotage will follow. Not only must you both contribute equally to the creation of the contract, the contract must also outline changes that will be made by both of you.

The Quid Pro Quo Contract

Now that you are clear on the basic requirements of a good contract, let's discuss the most popular form of intimate relationship contract: the Quid Pro Quo Contract. This type of contract produces the best outcomes due to its inherent mutuality. Both partners agree to make behavioral changes. For example, I promise to remind you once and only once to help Johnny with his homework. In return for my not nagging you, you agree to help Johnny for a half hour each night.

The benefit of this form of contracting—its mutuality—can also be its demise since both partners are expected to alter their behavior, score keeping can result. ("I did my part of the bargain three times and you held up your end only once.") If you or your partner are inclined to score keep, be very careful. In your case, it would be much better to frame the contract in terms of "I am making this change because I love you and want to keep the relationship."

The following is an example of a good contract: "For the next three weeks, I agree to wash the dishes on Monday, Wednesday, and Friday nights so that you can do your schoolwork. You agree to baby sit the kids on Tuesday and Thursday evenings, from seven to nine at night, and on Saturday mornings from eight to ten, so that I can attend my aerobics class. We agree to meet again on November 9 at noon to evaluate the success of this contract."

Put the Deal in Writing

So there is no room for confusion, it is best to commit your contracts to paper and post them conspicuously. By writing down your contracts, you lend a businesslike feel to the marriage. Some couples like this and others don't. The obvious advantage of a written contract is that it is less easy to weasel out of it. On the other hand, if your mate felt controlled as a kid, feeling obliged to write a contract down may give him a backed-into-the corner feeling, which could result in contract sabotage. So, rather than force your mate to write the contract down, discuss its pros and cons. Because the contract is mutual, and behavioral changes are promised on both sides, your mate should not feel too reluctant to commit it to paper. Remember, the written contract is for both of you, not just for him.

How Will We Know if the Contract is a Success?

Within the body of the contract, you both need to spell out the criteria you will use to evaluate the contract. Will feelings be the guide—that is, "The contract feels good to me, how about you?"? Will you judge the contract based upon ease of use? It is up to you both to decide. If you have decided to write your contract down, you will include the criteria for success or failure in the body of the contract.

When Will We Meet to Renegotiate?

The final feature of the contract is the provision for renegotiation. You both must agree on the date, time, and place at which you will get together to discuss whether the contract was a success or not. If one or both of you decide that the contract requires renegotiation, you will do so at the follow-up meeting. If you have decided to write your contract down, the follow-up date will be included. At the follow-up meeting, be prepared to conduct a new negotiation using the same steps as described above.

Handling a Common Negotiation Impasse

Endless Counterproposals

When negotiating, it is common for couples to become trapped in a net of counterproposals. (The, "I propose x, then I propose y syndrome.") When this occurs, you will find it impossible to "close" the deal. Endless counterproposals can arise when essential elements are missing from your contract. For example, if the contract is one-sided, as opposed to mutual, the overridden spouse may resist concluding the negotiation because the proposed plan doesn't take his own ideas into consideration.

Endless counterproposals can also conceal unspoken feelings. For example, a resistance to close the deal may conceal a fear of change or a fear that rocking the boat will only make the relationship worse. These fears may conceal an even deeper fear of being disappointed—if we arrive at a contract and my partner doesn't follow through, I'll be hurt.

Whenever counterproposals occur, it is good to explore your partner's thoughts regarding the meaning of the impasse. It is also imperative that both of you use your listening skills to thoroughly understand the feelings and objections to the various proposals on the table. Listening to each other's feelings is often sufficient to move the discussions forward.

Some Negotiation Examples

I'm going to give you a few examples of how various couples negotiated a resolution of their conflicts. In each example, I concentrate on one specific negotiation impasse, and show how the couple moved beyond it.

Example One

Negotiation Impasse: Poorly Constructed Problem Statement Leads to an Aborted Discussion.

Ester was annoyed that her husband always rushes sex. She told him many times, "I've seen animals wait longer!" No matter what Ester said or did, she has been unsuccessful in getting through to her husband, Pierre. She decided to try again, using my method.

She performed Self-Work and paid particular attention

to identifying their Old Scars. She realizes that his refusal to spend more time with her made her feel unloved, the way she did as a child. And as for Pierre, she recalled that he never felt that he lived up to his parents' expectations. She now realized why he had been so touchy whenever she had tried bring up their sexual problem.

She completed the remaining Self-Work tasks and then asked to talk.

She delivered her Ice Breaker, "Do you have a minute?" He was calculating the taxes and reluctantly looked up at her. (She had forgotten to Knock Before Entering and had approached him when he was busy. First mistake.)

Next, she stated her Lead-In, "I know you hate to talk about what I am going to say." (This is a statement of understanding, but not a positive, supportive statement.)

Then she said her Disclaimer, "And, I guess you don't mean to upset me," but... (The words, "I guess," sounded like she wasn't sure, which landed like an attack—"maybe you do mean to upset me.")

Next came the Presentation of the Issue (X, Y Formula): "But when you rush sex, I feel unloved." (She used the word "you," which heightened his feeling of being attacked.)

Then she added her Suggestion for the Future: "I want you to stop going so fast. (The suggestion was presented in a negative fashion, and it indirectly attacked him for going too fast.)

Pierre jumped up and stormed from the room.

"Oops. I guess I blew it," she said to herself.

She followed him and applied First Aid by saying, "I think I put you on the defensive. Can you tell me where I went wrong?"

He informed her and she told him that she would rethink her approach. They agreed to talk later that day.

200

When she reapproached, here's what she did:

She made sure to Knock Before Entering by saying: "Honey are you busy now? (He gave her the go ahead.)

She skipped the Ice Breaker (he already knew that there was a problem).

Next she stated her new and improved Lead-In, "I know how you felt put down by your parents, and that's the last thing that I want you to feel with me." (Mentioning his Old Scar; positioning herself as his friend and ally.)

Then she delivered her Disclaimer, "I know you don't realize the effect it has on me...but," which she followed by the Presentation of the Issue (the X, Y Formula), "when sex is over quickly, I feel unwanted." She omitted the word "you," and used very neutral phrasing.)

Then she added her Suggestion for the Future: "I want so much to spend more time being close and would value your suggestions on how we can pull this off." (The suggestion is presented in a positive fashion and leaves room for his input.)

Her new approach helped Pierre stay with the discussion and see it through to resolution.

Example Two

Negotiation Impasse: Husband Becomes Defensive after Problem Statement is Delivered.

Marian and Ed are standing in the bedroom embroiled in a boxer short battle. Each morning, Henry drops his underwear beside the bed, where it remains for days. History has shown that the underwear heap will become taller than Mount Rushmore if she doesn't break down and pick up after him.

Marian began by performing her Self-Work tasks. She focused first on understanding their Old Scars and soon realized that she was so angry with her husband because she had been treated like a maid in her first family. She also keyed in on the fact that Ed's mother bossed and controlled him. So as she prepared the words to kick off her discussion, she made a special effort to insure that he would not feel squashed by her.

Her Ice Breaker, Lead-In, Disclaimer and Problem Statement were as follows:

Ice Breaker: *"Honey, I need your advice on a problem. Do you have some time to talk to me now?"*

The Lead-In: *"You know how much I appreciate your problem-solving skills, and we need to take advantage of them now."*

The Disclaimer: *"I'm sure you don't mean to upset me, but..."*

Presentation of the Issue (X, Y Formula): *"When I have to pick up clothing from the floor, I feel so upset, the same way I felt when my family expected me to be the maid."*

Suggestion For the Future: (Keeping in mind that Ed becomes defensive when he feels told what to do, she presented her suggestion in an open-ended way, leaving room for his input.) *"I would like us to avoid this conflict in the future, and need your ideas on how we can do this."*

After she finished, Ed said, "Are you telling me that I'm a slob?" (defensive response)

She quickly applied First Aid. "Honey, you're not a slob. I'm just telling you how the laundry pile lands with me."

"You leave your stuff all over the house." (counter-blaming)

"You have a good point, and maybe we should talk about that later. (more First Aid)

After a few rounds of Cool-Down techniques, he settled down.

Next they began the negotiation process. Marian invited Ed to come up with ideas first. Initially he told her that late at night he was too tired to walk to the hamper in the laundry room. She listened to his feelings and told him that she understood. Feeling heard, he came up with a suggestion: that they move the hamper to the master bath—so that he could put the clothes in it each night, without feeling too put out. This solution was satisfactory to both partners. They committed the deal to paper and set a follow-up date to assess the contract.

Example Three

Negotiation Impasse: Husband's refusal to entertain his wife's suggestions, and his many counterproposals.

Connie rushed home, her arms loaded with a bag of Chinese food and a video. Doug promised to be home by seven. As usual, he was late. By eight o'clock, the dinner was stone-cold and she was boiling mad.

When Connie did her Self-Work, she discovered that feelings of hurt and terror were lurking beneath her anger. Her father, who was an alcoholic, often wouldn't return home for days, and, many times, she was frightened that he would never come home again. This explained why she was so upset when Doug came home late. As for Doug, Connie knew that his mother criticized him, and she realized that she needed to be very careful not to arouse his Old Scar.

After she completed all the Self-Work steps, she Knocked and delivered her Ice Breaker: "Doug, do you have some time to help me with a problem?"

When he agreed to talk right away, she stated her Lead-In: "I know how hard you work to support us."

Her Disclaimer: "And I know you don't realize the effect it has on me, but..."

Her Presentation of the Issue (the X, Y Formula): "When I am left wondering when you will come home, I am filled with terror, like when my dad stayed away."

Her Suggestion for the Future: "And I would feel so loved and safe, if I knew when you'd be home for dinner."

Doug was initially silent, but he did not become defensive. "I see what you mean," he finally said. Since he had received her issue, Connie asked whether he was ready to negotiate. He agreed.

She suggested that they set a later dinnertime, so that he would be sure to make it. Her proposal was met with refusal: "I can't say for sure when I'll be home." or with counterproposals that were not in tune with her request: "Instead of holding up dinner, why not eat without me?" She made five other suggestions and they all met with the same fate.

Connie suspected that his refusal and counterproposals were signs that ANS arousal was mounting. She decided to try a Cool-Down Question: "I notice that you keep rejecting my ideas. Do you know why?"

He said that her solutions seemed simplistic to him, and it felt like she was telling him that he was too dumb to think for himself. She listened, understood, and reflected her understanding back to him.

Having felt understood, he then came up with a suggestion. "The reason why I can't tell you when I'll be home is because the traffic on my route is unpredictable, and you know there aren't any public telephones on the country roads I drive. But, if I buy a cell phone, I'll be able to keep in touch with you all the time."

There was no need to commit their agreement to paper, or meet to renegotiate. The issue was resolved.

Having read the examples above, you may feel that the negotiation process is too involved or too difficult to put into practice. Have no fear. Each time you negotiate, it becomes easier and easier. If you can manage to hang in there and negotiate in this new way, however artificial or goofy it seems to you now, after approximately six weeks of doing so, you will find that what was once new will feel like old hat. So be patient. Put up with the emotional growing pains. You and your relationship will be eternally grateful you did.

Conclusion: Declaring a Permanent Truce

This conclusion contains a summary of the main principles outlined in this book. Warning: If you are reading this as a shortcut to reading the entire text, this book will self-destruct in three seconds. There are no quick fixes or Band-Aids for curing relationship conflict. You simply need to do the work. You need to learn the skills and techniques I've discussed and practice them until they become part of your bones. I know what I am suggesting is a pain, but your ongoing efforts will pay off. I promise you that.

What I want you to retain from chapter 1, your first Cool-Down step, is that heated exchanges cause ANS arousal and male withdrawal. Male withdrawal results in more heated exchanges, more ANS arousal and withdrawal, and a never ending, downward spiral of fighting. The point to remember is that your interactions must be cooled down before you can hope to achieve a resolution of your conflicts.

The second Cool-Down step, as I explained, is that before you can get control of your fights, you must figure out where you are in the Fighting Life Cycle. Stability of Conflict, or the Broken Record Phenomenon, is the primary clue that your fighting is out-of-control.

The third Cool-Down step is to help you identify your Fight Traps and faulty conflict resolution tactics. You need to remember that these traps and tactics heat the relationship climate, and that no conflict resolution can occur unless they are eliminated.

The fourth Cool-Down step is to resolve chronic sexual fights by teaching your partner to respond to your emotional needs, by understanding the differences between male and female sexuality, and, by identifying the nonsexual issues that are being played out in the sexual arena.

Cool-Down step 5 is to recognize that chronic marital fighting is usually caused by unresolved childhood wounds— Old Scars. The form your fights take clues you in to the nature of your Old Scars and the type of healing you need. As you heal your Old Scars within the relationship, you will pave the way for conflict resolution.

Cool-down step 6 is to train your mind to fight for you, not against you. Your cognitive distortions must be resolved before conflict resolution can occur.

The last Cool-Down step, number 7, is learning and using Relationship Climate Control techniques. The expressive nature of the female gender role ultimately triggers chronic fighting, and the only way to resolve this gender-driven impasse is through the use of these techniques to abort male withdrawal.

You are at last ready to begin my conflict resolution program. You must first acquire good listening skills, avoid the Listening Blunders, and resolve the Listening Blocks that cause them, all discussed in chapter 8.

The point to retain from chapter 9 is that before you learn to negotiate, you need to know when not to negotiate. Negotiating on inappropriate issues is counterproductive and, oftentimes, the source of greater relationship discord.

And, finally, it is time to negotiate a winning contract, but only after you have completed all the Self-Work tasks I described, and know how to introduce your issue for discussion. If a discussion leads on the wrong foot, it is doomed at the starting gate, and there will be no resolution.

The confronter must also remember to switch to discussion overseer, whose job it is to monitor for signs of ANS arousal and maintain a cool discussion that leads to a mutually satisfactory resolution of the conflict.

You've finally made it to the finish line! Wipe your sweaty brow. Breathe a sigh of relief, and give yourself a pat on the back. You have reached the end...and the beginning of a new life and a new relationship. I wish you much happiness and love.

References and Suggested Reading

1. Understanding the Chemistry of Fighting

Allen, J. G., and D. M Account, "Sex Differences in Emotionality: A Multidimensional Approach." *Human Relations* 29 (1976): 711-22.

Averill, J.R. "Studies on Anger and Aggression. Implications for Theories of Emotion." *American Psychologist* 38 no. 11 (1983): 1145-60.

Cannon, W.B. Bodily Changes in *Pain, Hunger, Fear and Rage: An Account of Researches into the Function of Emotional Excitement.* 2nd ed. New York: Appleton-Century-Crofts, 1929.

Gottmann, J. M. *Marital Interaction: Experimental Investigations.* New York: Academic Press, 1979.

Gottman, J.M., and R. W. Levenson, "The Social Psychophysiology of Marriage." In *Perspectives on Marital Interaction*, edited by P. Noller and M. A. Fitzpatrick, 182-202. Clevedon, Avon, England: Multilingual Matters, 1988.

Levenson, R. W., and J. M. Gottman, "Marital Interaction: Physiological Linkage and Affective Exchange." *Journal of Personality and Social Psychology* 45 (1983): 587-97.

Liberson, C. W., and W. T. Liberson. "Sex Differences in Autonomic Responses to Electric Shock." *Psychophysiology*

12 (1975): 182-86.

Mornell, P. *Passive Men, Wild Women.* New York: Ballantine Books, 1979.

Napier, A.Y. "The Rejection-Intrusion Pattern: A Central Family Dynamic." *Journal of Marriage and Family Counseling* 4 (1978): 5-12.

Notarius, C.I., and J. S.Johnson. "Emotional Expression in Husbands and Wives." *Journal of Marriage and the Family* 44 (1982): 483-89.

Notarius, C.I., and R.W. Levenson. "Expressive Tendencies and Physiological Responses to Stress." *Journal of Personality and Social Psychology* 37 (1979): 1204-10.

Roberts, L.J., and L. J Krokoff. "A Time-Series Analysis of Withdrawal, Hostility, Displeasure in Satisfied and Dissatisfied Marriages." *Journal of Marriage and the Family* 52 (1990): 95-105.

Turndorf, J. "Negative Affect Communication Deficits and the Demand/Withdraw Negative Escalation Cycle: A Psycho-Physiological Causal Pathway Model." Ph.D. in Psychology diss., California Coast University, 1994.

Van Doornen, L. J. P. "Sex Differences in Physiological Reactions to Real-Life Stress and Their Relationship to Psychological Variables." Paper presented at the 25th annual meeting of the Society for Psychophysiological Research, Houston, Texas, October 1985.

Zillmann, D. *Hostility and Aggression*. Hillsdale, N.J.: Lawrence Erlbaum, 1979.

2. The Relationship Battleground: Rate Your Conflicts on the Fighting Richter Scale

Ammons, P., and N. Stinnett. "The Vital Marriage: A Closer Look." *Family Relations* 29 (1980): 37-42.

Argyle, M., and A. Furnham.. "Sources of Satisfaction and Conflict in Long Term Relationships." *Journal of Marriage and the Family* 45 (1983): 481-93.

Baucom, D.H., and A.N. Adams. "Assessing Communication in Marital Interaction." In *Assessment of Marital Discord*, edited by K.D. O'Leary. Hillsdale, N.J.: Lawrence Erlbaum, 1987.

Billings, A. "Conflict Resolution in Distressed and Non-Distressed Married Couples." *Journal of Consulting and Clinical Psychology* 47, no. 2 (1979): 368-76.

Boyd, L. "Interpersonal Communication Skills Differentiating More Satisfying From less Satisfying Marital Relationships." Ph.D. diss., Texas A & M University, 1976.

Duck S. *Relating to Others*. Chicago: Dorsey, 1988.

Feldman, P. "Antagonistic Marriages." *Medical Aspects of Human Sexuality* 19 no. 11 (1985): 149-63.

Locke. H. J. *Predicting Adjustment in Marriage: A Comparison of a Divorced and a Happily Married group.* New York: Henry Holt & Co, 1951.

3. The No Fly (off the Handle) Zone: Eliminating Fight Traps and Faulty Conflict Resolution Tactics

Appel, M. S.; K.A. Holroyd, K.A.; and L. Gorkin. "Anger and the Etiology and Progression of Physical Illness." In *Emotions in Health and Illness: Theoretical and Research Foundations*, edited by L. Temoshok, C. VanDyke and L. S. Zegans. New York: Grune and Stratton, 1983.

Berger C. R. "Social Power and Interpersonal Communication." In *Handbook of Interpersonal Communication*, edited by M.L. Knapp and G.R. Miller, 439-99. Beverly Hills, CA: Sage, 1985.

Buunk, B. and C. Schaap. "Conflict Resolution Styles Attributed to Self and Partner in Premarital Relationships." *Journal of Social Psychology* 130, no. 6 (1990): 821-23.

Carter, B. and J.K. Peters. *Love, Honor and Negotiate: Making Your Marriage Work.* New York: Simon & Shuster, 1996.

Christensen, A. "Detection of Conflict Patterns in Couples." *In Understanding Major Mental Disorder: The Contribution of Family Interaction Research*, edited by K. Hahlweg and M. J. Goldstein. 250-65. New York: Family Process Press, 1987.

Fitzpatrick, M. A. "A Typological Approach to Marital Interaction." In *Perspectives on Marital Interaction*, 98-120. Clevedon, Avon, England: Multilingual Matters, 1988.

Goldberg, M. "Patterns of Disagreement in Marriage." *Medical Aspects of Human Sexuality* 21, no. 3 (1987): 42-52.

Sullaway, M., and A. Christensen. "Assessment of Dysfunctional Interaction Patterns in Couples." *Journal of Marriage and the Family* 45 (1983): 653-660.

4.Battle of the Bulge: The Sex Wars

Balswick, J., and C. Peek. "The Inexpressive Male: A Tragedy of American Society." *The Family Coordinator* 20 (1971): 363-68.

Coleman, M., and L. H. Ganong. "Love and Sex Role Stereotypes: Do Macho Men and Feminine Women Make Better Lovers?" *Journal of Personality and Social Psychology* 49 (1985): 170-76.

Jourard, S. M., and P. Lasakow. "Some Factors in Self-Disclosure." *Journal of Abnormal and Social Psychology* 56 (1958): 91-98.

Rubin, L.B. *Intimate Strangers: Men and Women Together.* New York: Harper & Row, 1983.

5. Battle Scars: How Childhood Wounds Cause Chronic Conflict and How to Heal Them

Bell, E. C., and R. N. Blakeney. "Personality Correlates of Conflict Resolution Modes." *Human Relations* 30 (1977): 849-57.

Bradshaw, J. *Homecoming: Reclaiming and Championing Your Inner Child.* New York: Bantam Books, 1990.

6. How Your Head Can Be Your Own Worst Enemy: Training Your Mind to Fight For (Not against) You

Baucom, D. H. "Attributions in Distressed Relations: How Can We Explain Them?" *In Intimate Relationships: Development, Dynamics and Deterioration,* edited by Daniel Perlman and Steve Duck Steve. Beverly Hills, CA: Sage, 1987.

Beck, A. T. *Cognitive Therapy and Emotional Disorders.* New York: International Universities Press, 1976.

Borysenko, J. *Guilt is the Teacher, Love is the Lesson.* New York: Warner Books, 1990.

Burns, D. D. *The Feeling Good Handbook: Using the New Mood Therapy in Everyday Life.* New York: William Morrow, 1989.

7.The Battle Ax: How Women Can Use Climate Control Techniques to End Relationship Fighting

Gottman, J.M., and L. J. Krokoff. "Marital Interaction and Satisfaction: A longitudinal View." *Journal of Consulting and Clinical Psychology* 57 (1989): 47-52.

Gottman, J.M., and N. Silver. *Why Marriages Succeed or Fail...And How You Can Make Yours Last.* New York: Simon & Shuster, 1995.

Hendrix, H. *Getting the Love You Want.* New York: Henry Holt, 1988.

8. Listening To The Battle Cry: How to Use Your Ears to Resolve Conflicts

Buck, R. *The Communication of Emotion.* New York: Guilford, 1984.

Buck, R. "Nonverbal Behavior and the Theory of Emotion: The Facial Feedback Hypothesis." *Journal of Personality and Social Psychology* 30 (1980): 811-24.

Jourard, S. M., and P. Lasakow. "Some Factors in Self-Disclosure." *Journal of Abnormal and Social Psychology* 56 (1958): 91-8.

Noller, P. *Nonverbal Communication and Marital Interaction.* New York: Pergamon, 1984.

Resolution with Couples." *Journal of Reality Therapy* 8, no. 1 (1988): 7-12.

Rusbalt, C. E., D. J. Johnson; and G. D. Morrow "Impact of Couple Patterns of Problem Solving on Distress and Nondistress in Dating Relationships." *Journal of Personality and Social Psychology* 50 (1986): 744-53.

9. On Furlough: Knowing When Not to Negotiate

Buck, R. *The Communication of Emotion*. New York: Guilford, 1984.

10. The Peace Treaty: How to Negotiate a Contract

Alexander, J. F. "Defensive and Supportive Communications in Family Systems." *Journal of Marriage and the Family* 35 (1973): 613-617.

Billings, A. "Conflict Resolution in Distressed and Non-Distressed Married Couples." *Journal of Consulting and Clinical Psychology* 47, no. 2 (1979): 368-76.

Folger, J.P., and M. S. Poole. *Working Through Conflict*. Glenview, Ill.: Scott Foresman, 1984.

Gottman, J. M. "Emotional Responsiveness in Marital Conversations." *Journal of Communication* 16 (1982): 108-19.

Hallock, S. "An Understanding of Negotiation Styles

Contributes to Effective Reality Therapy for Conflict Resolution with Couples." *Journal of Reality Therapy* 8, no. 1 (1988): 7-12.

Rusbalt, C. E.,; D. J. Johnson; and G. D. Morrow "Impact of Couple Patterns of Problem Solving on Distress and Nondistress in Dating Relationships." *Journal of Personality and Social Psychology* 50 (1986): 744-53.

Index

domestic violence, 4

echo process, 100
emotional connection breaker blunders, 132
emotional core, assessing, 167
emotional course of a fight, charting, 76
emotional levels, changing, 135
emotional providers, husbands and male partners as, 60
emotional right-of-way, 190
emotional states as nonnegotiable issues, 159, 170
emotional type of communications. *See* listening to the battle
    cry
emotional understanding, conveying, 122
emotional venting, 26, 178
ending relationship fighting by women using climate control
    techniques, 106, 207
  acceptance of differences, 118
  ANS arousal and, 107
  benefit of the doubt giving and, 110
  calm tone and, 112
  communications and, 110
  conveying emotional understanding, 122
  elements of, 107
  exercises to partially identify with mate's feelings for,
    129
  five-to-one ratio and, 110, 119
  general techniques for, 111
  global accusations and, 127
  humor of, 116
  keeping promises for, 123
  knowing when to shut up and, 108
  letting it go and, 108
  meeting each others needs and, 117